A To
OLD TASMANIA

with

Michael Tatlow
Charles Wooley

and

Peter Mercer

WALK GUIDES AUSTRALIA

THE COVER

TOURING TASMANIA was an occasion for wearing your best duds in the late 1800s. Here a bunch of likely lads is coaching from Hobart to the Huon Valley. A coach load of lady tourists, we understand, went ahead of them, evidently unphotographed. Photo from Black & White Photographics, Launceston.

First published December 2008

© Walk Guides Australia 2008

Designed by Michael Tatlow

Graphic art by Peter Bublyk. peterbub@hotmail.com

Printed by Graphic Impressions. www.gimpressions.com.au

ISBN 978-0-9805637-3-3

Modern photography, unless otherwise credited, by Michael Tatlow

Thanks

A vital contributor to this book was John Piggott, General Manager of Walk Guides Australia. Our thanks go to Peter Mercer's wife and historian, Libby, who selflessly helped. We thank photographer-historian Tony Hope (author of the book *A Quarry Speaks: A History of Hobart's Salamanca Quarry*) and Colin Dennison of Hobart and Peter Clark (Black & White Photography, Launceston) whose vast collections of old photographs we have drawn on.

Derwent Valley Mayor Tony Nicholson and historian Colin Jones, the Mayor of the West Coast Darryl Gerrity, the Deputy Mayor of Clarence Doug Chipman, and Stanley's Marguerite Eldridge told us a lot about their patches. Many other people enthusiastically helped us. They include name-origins specialist and author Wayne Smith, historian Reg A. Watson, Cornwall's Jim Haas, George Town historian Des Wootton, West Tamar historian Helen Phillips, researcher about Chinese miners Trevor Rootes, Hobart's Lewis Wooley, Mim Baly and Cal Walker of Wynyard and David Cripps of Hobart.

We particularly thank our advertisers, whose investments made it possible to sell this book so cheaply.

Your authors

THEY HAVE strong connections with Tasmania and know it well.

Michael Tatlow and Charles Wooley are noted journalists who co-wrote this book's sister publications *A Walk in Old Sydney*, *A Walk in Old Hobart* and *A Walk in Old Launceston*, long-time and still top sellers in Tasmania when this book was printed. The books have been praised by historians, reviewers and tourism professionals. Pre-eminent historian Peter Mercer was the books' vital checker for accuracy.

1920s tourers of Tasmania.
Black & White Photographics, Launceston.

Latter-day tourers, Charlie, Mike and Peter. Photo: Tony Briscoe.

MICHAEL TATLOW is a former national newspaper and television journalist who, like Charles, is also a world traveller. He is a sixth-generation Tasmanian. His ancestors lived on the North West Coast, in Launceston and Hobart from the 1820s. Michael was a journalist with *The Advocate* in Burnie and *The Examiner* in Launceston before advancing a career with newspapers and television in Sydney, where he became Chief of Staff of the *Daily Telegraph*, and News Editor of *The Sunday Telegraph* and *The Bulletin*. Back in the cloister of his native isle, Michael wrote the thriller novel *Pike's Pyramid* (ISBN 0-9802814-1-5 published 2006), which dramatically showcases Tasmania.

CHARLES WOOLEY is a national celebrity journalist who spent much of his youth in the pioneering Tasmanian villages of Tarraleah and Rossarden and then in Launceston after coming to Tasmania as a toddler with his parents from the Scots isle of Arran in the Irish Sea. His keen interest in Tasmania's colourful heritage and protecting its environment inspired his collaboration with Michael to produce the series of books including this latest work.

After many years of globetrotting as a reporter for the *Sixty Minutes* television program, Charles is qualified to rate Tasmania as the most remarkable and magnificent place in the world to visit. While continuing as an occasional television presenter and reporter, he now hosts from Hobart the daily radio program *Charles Wooley Across Australia* to 40 radio stations on Macquarie Regional Radio. Charles' book *Travelling Tales* (ISBN 0-09-182977-1) is a collection of rattling and hilarious yarns about his trotting around the globe.

PETER MERCER, OAM, is a revered historian who has been a resident of Launceston and Burnie and now lives in Hobart. Peter was a long-time Senior Curator of History at the Tasmanian Museum and Art Gallery in Hobart and received the Order of Australia for his contribution to preserving, researching and recording Tasmania's rich heritage. An enduring and popular legacy of Peter is the Pioneer Village Museum in Burnie, which he created and founded. It is visited on our Tours. His books on Tasmanian history include three on Burnie including *Burnie – its history and development* and *Gateway to Progress: the Centenary History of the Marine Board of Burnie*. Others include *A Most Dangerous Occupation* (Runnymede's whaling connection) and *Built for a Merchant* (history of Narryna.). He is also the author of more than 300 learned papers and articles on Tasmanian history, built heritage and social history. Peter is an honorary life member of the National Trust of Australia (Tasmania).

FOREWORD, by Peter Cundall

A guide we needed

A WELCOME strength of this book is that it takes visitors to our State to lesser-known regional areas of enchantment as well as to our main tourism centres.

I also welcome the authors' decision to donate a goodly percentage from the sale of the book to the urgent and vital program to help save the Tasmanian Devil from extinction.

Reading *A Tour of Old Tasmania* will comprehensively confirm that this island of such compact physical contrasts has as much to offer during a motoring, biking or walking tour for a week or a month or more as any other spot on earth.

Michael Tatlow, Charles Wooley and Peter Mercer are accomplished Tasmanians who have made a considerable contribution to the appreciation and awareness of our island's remarkable natural beauty and built heritage with this book in the wake of their highly popular books *A Walk in Old Hobart* and *A Walk in Old Launceston*.

The authors have written this work with candid authority, bringing to life colonial characters and events with splashes of pathos and comedy. Their pages also demonstrate the urgent importance of preserving Tasmania's old forests and wildlife, and of keeping it free of pollutants.

This is a much needed book, which lets visitors know that you need more than a few days' motoring to see much of Tasmania at all. It will also entertain and enlighten residents of our island.

Tempting as it is to keep it a secret, do tell your friends at home about terrific Tassie. And we'd like to see you back again.

Peter Cundall

◁ Contents ▷

Summer reflections. Black Angus drinks break near Melton Mowbray in the Midlands.

The Big Tree reserve in the Valley of the Giants by the Styx River, north-west of New Norfolk. Its cathedral of eucalypts are the world's oldest and tallest. Can you see the woman between the giants? Photo by Geoff Law, The Wilderness Society.

Welcome to our enchanted isle

YOUR AUTHORS are Tasmanians who know this island well. We treasure its striking difference! So preciously different from the rest of Australia. So sublimely different from other places in the world. The scenic diversity packed into our island is unparalleled.

This book shows you how to tour it in a week, a few weeks or for a month or so, travelling a lot of byways to little-appreciated gems with minimal backtracking. And it reveals many local secrets.

You do not have to take the Tour to enjoy this uniquely-presented history of Tasmania. But, even if you are a resident of the island, we tip that after reading it you will want to.

This book attends importantly to the questions that commonly confront new visitors: Where should we go? How much can we see in a leisurely way in our week or month here? What is the best way to explore Tasmania's rich heritage?

Our recommended tours encourage casual motoring, rather than driving. Along the way, we also suggest many side trips to places of special fascination. To know what awaits, we suggest that you read the relevant chapter before going on that part of the Tour.

The tours allow plenty of time to take in the flavour of the place, to smell the flowers. Importantly, we want you to meet the locals and explore scores of links with Tasmania's romantic, at times tough and turbulent, history to which our text and photographs give prominence.

Snapshot narratives capture stirring, dramatic and comic moments in history to give you a graphic taste of the times.

Tasmania looks to be a little pipsqueak of a place on a map, shaped like a heart nestling under mainland Australia, that you could see most of in a week. Not so. It is nearly as big as Ireland. And it is such a geological wonder of a place, with hills and mountains everywhere you look, punctuated by lush meadows, forested valleys and plateaus with mountain trout-streams and lakes. Just south of the world's flattest continent, incidentally. We reckon that if its 64,500 square kilometres were magically flattened the island would be bigger than New South Wales! Well, nearly.

Looking at Tasmania in an atlas, next stop Antarctica, can suggest it is a bleak place. Not so, again. Its climate is like that of the south of France. Snow is common in the highlands in winter but temperatures often go above 30 degrees Celsius in summer. Although nearby Mt Wellington regularly has a white cap, snow settles in Hobart once every 20 years or so. Unlike, say, Athens; with snow most winters. Hobart is as close to the equator as Rome and Barcelona.

A banquet of beauty

YOU CAN GET only a small taste of this enchanting isle, a sort of tasty entrée, motoring around for a week, as covered on our recommended East Coaster tour. The West Coaster takes a week or so longer and is more like a main course.

For the full feast, laden with stunning side dishes, come with us if you have the time, right around, through and over Tasmania for a meandering month or more of marvels on our Grand Tour.

Every tour is presented with its own map showing the route in red and we have kept back-tracking to a minimum. Recommended side trips are marked in blue.

The East Coaster and West Coaster routes cover much of the Grand Tour. So, if you do not have time on this visit to Tasmania for the full works, you can take a shorter course and complete the banquet on your next holiday. We know you will want to come back.

Our tour also visits many of Tasmania's countless islands; notably Bruny, Flinders, King, Maria and even the former isle of hell for convicts, Sarah, on the West Coast. This, after all, is a State of islands rather than an island State.

Most tourers of Tasmania arrive at Devonport on the ships *Spirit of Tasmania* I and II. As well as ferrying some 150,000 resident Tasmanians, the ships bring about 250,000 tourists to Tasmania a year. Not bad for a place with a population nearing 500,000.

Our chosen tour narratives travel the State clockwise. They begin and conclude at Devonport. But, of course, thousands of visitors fly in, mostly to Hobart, Launceston, Wynyard or Devonport, and hire or borrow cars, campervans and caravans. So you can easily begin and finish at these places.

The tours are fine, of course, for motor bikers, cyclists and backpackers. Most of the roads on the main tours are sealed but some of our suggested side trips are on gravel roads in good condition, at least as we write this. Every suggested road along the way is okay for two-wheel drive vehicles.

As so many local historians have staunchly told us, the stories of their towns merit individual thick volumes. We hope they will understand our need here for brevity.

The isle of contrasts ... Walls of barely-penetrable trees and bushes on the lush West Coast near Tullah almost turn the Murchison Highway into a tunnel.

The Great Aussie Outback? No, our route through sheep-grazing land in the upper Midlands, north-west of Campbell Town. Photo: Charles Wooley.

Ask around

WE HAVE presented this book assuming that you call at Travel and Information Centres throughout your tour. At these you can soak up local knowledge about what to see, what is in the district to nourish your culinary or cultural or recreational preferences, find out where to stay, and collect local maps, brochures and booklets about local attractions. The information centres' locations are shown on our maps with distinctive, yellow "i" signs. The network is supported by municipal councils and tourism promoters with help from Tourism Tasmania. The island also has a host of info. centres run by volunteers, who usually include local history buffs. Some do not bother, but many are identified by "i" signs painted white. Yes, they're known as White Eyes. And, of course, don't hesitate to ask for directions from the locals.

Tasmania's population is more decentralised than in any other Australian State. There are inevitably hundreds of back roads, often going to enchanting little villages and beauty spots that are not part of our recommended tours. It would takes months to explore all of them. So if you see an inviting track that your vehicle can handle and you have the time, go for it! This gem of the south is packed with rewarding surprises.

Enjoy our pristine air and the unique light artists value so much. We natives, you will find, are pretty friendly. We value your presence in Tasmania. We hope you have a wonderful time and that you return.

Travel distances

THE CHAPTER-LIKE PARTS of our tours are not necessarily presented as one-day excursions. They end at ideal overnight locations, though, whether you stay at hotels or b. & bs or are camping. You may like to spend several days on some stages. Others can be covered in a few hours if your time is limited.

THE GRAND TOUR is a circuit of the island, including the northern, eastern, southern and western coasts, the Midlands and the majestic Highlands. See the map on page 10. You go to nearly every community we rate to have significant historical interest. We suggest taking three to six weeks to complete it. The Grand Tour is divided into 16 parts of 80 to 220 km, covering a total of 2,150 km. Taking most of our recommended side trips will add a further 500 km or so, giving a round tour of Tasmania of some 2,700 km. If you have plenty of overnight breaks along the way, take all the side trips and spend 20 days travelling, you will cover an average of a casual 135 km a day.

THE WEST COASTER covers more than half of the Grand Tour. The map is on page 227. It loops from Devonport, through Launceston and the Midlands to Port Arthur, the Huon south of Hobart, the marvellous Derwent Valley and the Valley of the Giants, lakes in the Highlands and the splendour of the West Coast and the far North West including Stanley. The tour covers 1,795 kms divided into 11 parts of 80 to 335 kms each.

Not including a further 300 km for some of our suggested side trips, in 10 days of travelling you will average a relaxing 180 km a day. You could rush around the West Coaster in a week, but to get the most from this superb Tour allow three weeks.

THE EAST COASTER, covering nearly half of the Grand Tour on easy roads in warmer parts of the island, is ideal for a holiday of one to two weeks. The map is on page 223. From Devonport and Launceston, it covers the wondrous Tamar River Valley, the island's leading wine-growing areas, the East Coast's beaches and pink-granited Coles Bay, Port Arthur, Hobart and the Midlands. A little-known stop on the East Coast takes you (as does the Grand Tour) into what we call Little Gondwana, a magical valley of pre-history that the ravages of time seem to have bypassed.

The East Coaster does not include the Highlands and the West Coast, where some roads can be treacherous in winter. It covers 1,385 kms, presented in 11 parts of between 40 and 220 kms each. Not including a further 300 kms for some of our side trips, in seven days of travelling you will cover a daily average of 200 kms.

Home sweet home. A Highlands bushman proudly showing off his bark hut in the late 1800s.

Companions for the trip

Visit our website www.walkguidesaustralia.com for more information. From there you can also buy copies of this book, *A Walk in Old Sydney*, *A Walk in Old Hobart* and a *Walk in Old Launceston*.

The site also tells you about *A Walk in Old Hobart* and *A Walk in Old Launceston*. Both of them are stand-out top sellers to visitors and Tasmanian residents alike, praised by reviewers and tourism professionals and historians. They are essential companions if you want to get to really know Tasmania's two main and amazing cities, the second and third oldest in Australia, warts and all. Do go to the site and tell us about your tour.

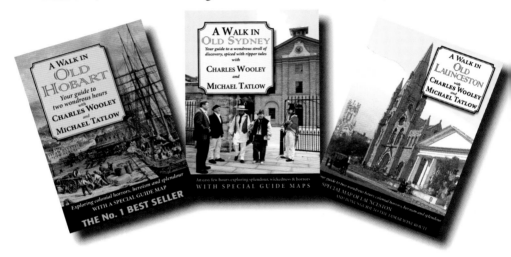

A Brief History of Tasmania

ONLY ABOUT 5,000 ABORIGINES in perhaps 70 tribal groups in nine different regional divisions had lived in a stone-age way in Tasmania for some 40,000 years when Dutch mariner Abel Janszoon Tasman, with two ships, discovered the island in 1642 after battling the storm-tossed Southern Ocean. He named it Van Diemen's Land after his boss in Batavia, now Jakarta.

The first Tasmanians spoke five different languages, so they did not mix much. They seem to have been different racially from natives in the mainland States. They were probably the first Australians, driven south by

Aborigines in Tasmania in 1859, Robert Dowling's collage from old portraits of tribal leaders by Thomas Bock. The original is in the Queen Victoria Museum and Art Gallery, Launceston.

waves of later arrivals from the north. They were isolated when the last ice age ended, sea levels rose, and their homeland became an island 10,000 years ago.

A motley group from Sydney, led by an English sailor, landed with convicts, soldiers and a few farmer settlers on the eastern shore of the River Derwent in September 1803. A second party established a penal settlement across the river at Hobart Town in February 1804. Expeditioners with more convicts settled by the Tamar River, downstream from today's Launceston, nine months later.

Instances of murderous brutality towards the first Tasmanians, but mainly European diseases, caused the extinction of full-blooded Aborigines in less than a generation. Indigenous animals such as the dog-like striped marsupial thylacine (the Tasmanian tiger) lasted well into the 1900s and the small Tasmanian emu became extinct about 1850.

Animals including rabbits, hares, starlings, sparrows and (we must admit) the marvellous trout, along with blackberries, gorse, hawthorn and European trees and flowers were introduced to remind the pioneers of England.

Some 67,000 convicts were transported to Van Diemen's Land from Sydney and directly from England and Ireland, often for piddling offences such as stealing an apple. Also incarcerated were Canadian, American and New Zealand Maori freedom fighters. Some were treated brutally at prisons such as Sarah Island in Macquarie Harbour on the West Coast, Maria Island on the East Coast and later in the "model prison" at Port Arthur. But most of them fared better eventually than they would have in the slums of Dublin and London.

About 14,000 convicts were women and many were boys and girls, some as young as six. Most of the convicts worked on road gangs, cleared forests for farming, quarried and cut stone for buildings, and were assigned to be slave-like labourers and servants for pseudo aristocrats who established their shallow roots on estates granted by governors. At least one in four of today's Tasmanians are convicts' descendants.

Apart for some early days of deprivation, settlements thrived around the fertile and, later to prove, mineral-rich island, endowed with a temperate climate and plenty of water. About 540 convicts were hanged, however. Treadmills and law breakers bolted into stocks for public shaming and abuse were part of colonial Hobart and Launceston. Bushrangers, mostly escaped convicts, marauded widely.

The British colony's name was changed to Tasmania in 1856, three years after the end of convict transportation, in an effort to banish the "convict stain" and in remarkable recognition of the Dutch discoverer of the island compared with the royalist and English names of Victoria, Queensland and New South Wales.

Whaling and sealing, timber getting, productive farming and fishing and later mineral mining drove diversified industrial development and exports through the 1800s. The economy was enriched into the 1900s as people around the world learned of the wonders of Tasmania and slowly began what is today's tourism boom.

In the wake of World War II mass immigration by Europeans in the 1950s and 60s, notably of people from Mediterranean and Baltic countries and later Asians and Africans, enriched and diversified lifestyles.

Tasmania's heritage register lists 5,500 built structures. Two thirds of all 19th century buildings on the Commonwealth heritage database are on this island. Tasmanians today are the nation's keenest readers of books. It is the home of distinguished writers and artists and composers and actors, of sophisticated diners and of the makers of some of the world's finest wines, cheeses, chocolates, beer, whisky, furniture, musical instruments and even ships. We produce wasabi for Japan, tulips for Holland, ginseng for Asia, truffles for France and smoked Atlantic salmon for everyone.

Our only significant disharmony is between Tasmanians who favour and Tasmanians who oppose the extent of clear-felling of native forests and the associated killing of native animals, mostly to sustain the wood-chip exporting industry.

Sure, some awful things happened along the way. But quite a rise, it's been, from the raw degradation of Tasmanian society in those pioneering days only a couple of hundred years ago.

Hobart Town, Van Diemen's Land, from the (now) Royal Botanical Gardens in 1828. This was about 30 years before today's Parliament House was built where the workers are. Aquatint by R. G. Reeve after G. W. Evans. Old Tasmanian Prints, Clifford Craig.

TASMANIA

Love this place®

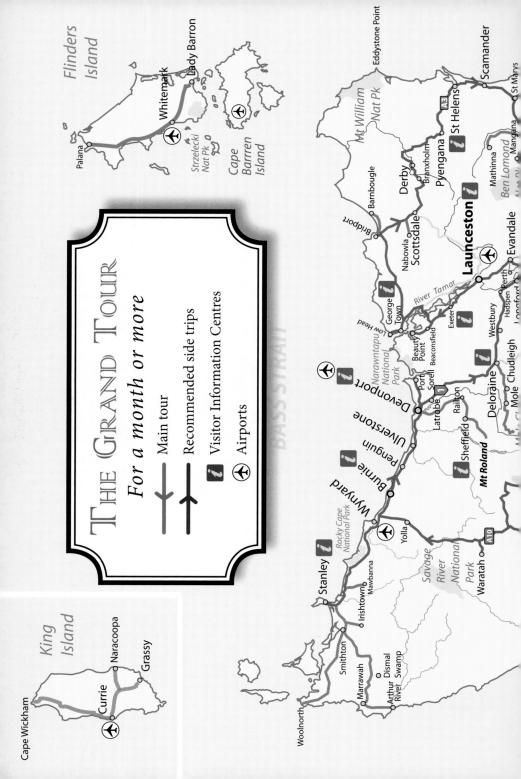

The Grand Tour

For a month or more

— Main tour

— Recommended side trips

ℹ Visitor Information Centres

✈ Airports

Flinders Island

Palana
Whitemark
Lady Barron
Strzelecki Nat Pk
Cape Barren Island

King Island

Cape Wickham
Currie
Naracoopa
Grassy

BASS STRAIT

Woolnorth
Smithton
Marrawah
Arthur Dismal River Swamp
Irishtown
Mawbanna
Stanley ℹ
Rocky Cape National Park
Yolla
Waratah
Savage River National Park
Wynyard ✈
Burnie ℹ
Penguin
Ulverstone
Sheffield ℹ
Mt Roland
Devonport ✈ ℹ
Narawntapu National Park
Port Sorell
Latrobe
Railton
Deloraine ℹ
Mole Chudleigh
A10
Beauty Point
Beaconsfield
Exeter
Westbury
Low Head
George Town ℹ
River Tamar
Launceston ✈ ℹ
Perth
Hadspen
Longford
Evandale
Ben Lomond Nat Pk
Bridport
Barnbougle
Nabowla
Scottsdale ℹ
Derby
Branxholm
Pyengana
St Helens ℹ
A3
Mathinna
Mangana
St Marys
Scamander
Eddystone Point
Mt William Nat Pk

© Walk Guides Australia

Scale 1:2 000 000

0   25   50km

THE GRAND TOUR. 2,150 KM

Although our tour narrative begins and ends at Devonport, the circular course means that you can begin and finish this and our other tours anywhere along the way. Enjoy!

The Mersey River about 1910, from near today's bridge. Colin Dennison Collection.

PART ONE 160 km
Devonport, Latrobe, Deloraine, Longford, Evandale, Launceston

A SAND BAR BLOCKING the mouth of the river and a tall forest on the fertile soil on its banks made the site of today's **Devonport** hard to see, and harder for early explorers to sail to. For a long time settlers stayed away, put off from this lush part of the world by a clot of an explorer who sailed by on a surveying mission in 1823.

Naval Lieutenant Charles Hardwicke reckoned to the governor that this region was "mountainous, extremely barren and totally unfit for habitation".

So the Aborigines whose ancestors had lived here for some 40,000 years remained undisturbed until Edward Curr, the chief agent for the Van Diemen's Land Company, was impressed when he came

Devonport on the Mersey 1874. View from where the Spirit of Tasmania *ships berth today. A. W. Marshall photo, Colin Dennison Collection.*

looking for grazing land in 1826 and named the Mersey River after the stream at his former home town; Liverpool, England.

With only bush tracks for a long time, most people and provisions went to the Mersey by sea. The first village from 1851 was Torquay, now East Devonport, where the *Spirits of Tasmania* berth. Across the river, the settlements of Formby and Wenvoe followed a few years later. A couple of generations had to swim or take a boat over the Mersey until a bridge opened in 1902, a year after the federation of Australia. A prosperous little timber-getting settlement by the Don River, some five kilometres west with a sawmill and tramway, drove the local economy until the mid 1800s.

Victoria's gold rush in the early 1850s created a strong market for timber, food and other provisions from the Mersey and other northern ports. Convicts wanting to flee the colony also welcomed the boom. The surge of shipping to Melbourne gave them a good way of escape. Scores of desperate men and women did just this until Victoria in 1853 made it a serious crime to take convicts across then Bass's Strait.

After fiery renaming debate between the supporters of the villages sundered by the river, Devonport and Devonport East became official in 1890. This was five years into a second boom brought by the completion of the railway line from Deloraine to the Mersey heads. It crossed the river way upstream. Construction of today's lighthouse on the Bluff and the clearing of the sandbar also fuelled rapid development.

Pioneer farmer James Fenton at nearby Forth took the blame for planting six cuttings of imported blackberries, which, like imported gorse and Scotch thistle, created the rampant blots on the landscape which we have today. To his credit, Fenton also introduced clover. He was the first in the island to copy the Canadian practice of ring-barking trees, enabling the killing of forest giants to farm the land without having to chop them down. Pasture among forests of dead, ring-barked trees was the typical landscape in this part of the island until the early 1900s.

It might look more like an industrial centre than a tourist mecca at first if you have arrived on the *Spirit of Tasmania*, but do see the gem of a city across the river. It is the State's third biggest (pop. 26,000) in a coastal setting bordered by some of the richest farmland in the nation. If only Lieutenant Charles Hardwicke could see the "extremely barren" place today …

We suggest at first a side trip from East Devonport past Pardoe airport to Hawley Beach and peaceful **Port Sorell** by the mouth of the Rubicon River. The town, originally called Burgess in 1844, was the early settlement and port for this part of the North-West Coast. Port Sorell was named after the colony's third Lieutenant Governor, William Sorell, like scores of places on our Tour named after governors.

The Van Diemen's Land Company's Edward Curr tried to establish the district's first farming enterprise here in 1826. But Lieut. Governor Arthur soon sent the company packing west up the coast to Circular Head. In 1831 Aborigines of the Big River Tribe speared and clubbed to death the property's second owner Captain Bartholomew Thomas and James Parker, his overseer.

Back at East Devonport, cross the bridge over the Mersey and travel to the right along Formby Road to the well-signed Visitor Information Centre for accommodation information and for directions to local heritage attractions such as the Regional Art Gallery and Home Hill, the gracious former home of a great Tasmanian family: Tasmania's sole Australian Prime Minister, Joe Lyons, his Federal MP wife Dame Enid and their 11 surviving children. Memorabilia there makes it a national shrine.

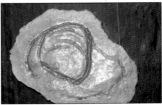

A reproduced Devonport Bluff Aboriginal rock carving at the Tiagarra Aboriginal Centre.

From the CBD, continue north on Victoria Parade beside gardens, fine old residences and the Mersey. The Maritime Museum, at the former harbour master's residence near the heads, has a splendid showcase of nautical history you should see. Victoria Parade becomes Bluff Road, going a couple of kms by the coast to the city's small beach. A right turn here takes you to Mersey Bluff, with its outstanding, powered camping ground.

Devonport's first ferry? Passengers crossing the Mersey c. 1855 paid a penny. The main building at (now) East Devonport was the Victoria Hotel. Black & White Photographics.

At the Bluff's summit, with views east and west along the coast, is the old lighthouse and the Tiagarra Aboriginal Centre. From here you can find out about the first Tasmanians who lived on this coastline. They left behind a bounty of carvings in large rocks of diminishing circles and various shapes. Co-author Michael Tatlow discovered and reported the presence of some of these petroglyphs when he lived near the then-overgrown Bluff as a teenager. (It's a shameful thing to confess now, but he was building a collection of birds' eggs.) Your Devonport exploration could continue along the coast, past Coles Beach, to the Don River Heads.

Wharfies about 1910, soon after trains came to Devonport, loading bags of potatoes. The spuds came from the rich countryside declared "extremely barren". Stephen Spurling photo, Colin Dennison Collection.

SNAPSHOT 1863

A passage to freedom

A FRESH BREEZE sweeping up the Mersey from the sea carries a salty tang on a September afternoon in 1863. In this snapshot of that day, imagine that you are at the little wharf at Torquay, where the *Spirit of Tasmania* berths today.

You have crossed the Mersey on the punt ferry for the price of one penny to watch the loading of the little schooner *Cousins*. Hessian bags of potatoes are being hefted from a farm dray drawn by a blinkered heavy shire horse to the hold of the 41-footer.

This is the liveliest sight in the settlement today. *Cousins* has become a regular caller. She was built, you know, at the mouth of Supply Creek on the Tamar River 16 years ago for brothers James and John Cartledge, who owned the flour-mill there. Her deck is crowded with timber, cloth, spring vegetables and beef and mutton in casks of brine for hungry and gold-rich Victoria.

Four men in tattered clothing are feverishly loading a rowing skiff near you with picks and shovels, pans, home-made sieves and muskets.

"Why go for gold at Bendigo?" one says to a trim young lady, a farmer's wife of your acquaintance, sitting at the front of the dray. "There's rich minerals, gold or silver we hope, up the river as well as the coal found there. We're going on the tide tonight. Way past Latrobe. Into the never never. The guns are to get our tucker." He takes a bite of chewing tobacco. "We're going to be rich men, ma'am, *rich*!"

She wishes them good fortune, turns and resumes a study of a young man and a red-haired girl in her late teens standing stiffly, but hand in hand. They are in the shade of a shed near *Cousins*. The youth holds a small sack. Their sole possessions? you wonder.

The fair lady must have noted the couple's look of desperation, their ragged clothes. She has picked them for runaways, you reckon, probably children of convicts, perhaps eloping, hungering for new lives in prosperous Melbourne. All roads lead to Melbourne, city of gold. It seems they are victims of the long depression plaguing this colony. They look to be summoning the courage to ask for working passages across the Strait, perhaps wondering how to stow away.

The lady who is dispatching her potatoes would know Captain Holyman, who bought *Cousins* a year past for close to 100 pounds. You are quietly aware that Holyman, a sailor who jumped ship in Launceston nine years ago, plans to have his own shipping line. He is a kindly man with a tough job, now on the deck checking the balance of the load in his small craft. Every corner safely stowed is money to him.

The lady smiles towards the couple. Then she smartly walks up the gangplank and addresses the captain.

"William, see that lovely young couple over there? I believe they want for the fare to Melbourne. Could they join your crew? Work their passage?"

The skipper hesitates, then smiles and nods. The lady beckons to the attentive couple, calling them on board. The youth self-consciously shakes the captain's hand. They give their names in lilting Irish brogues.

"I can cook and scrub, sir, and my husband has sailed on the Irish sea," the girl presses. As Captain Holyman directs them below decks, she steps forward and hugs her lady helper. Beaming now, the couple face freedom from want. As she begins to descend to the galley, the girl turns again to her advocate and the skipper. "Oh, God bless you, sir and milady."

The prospectors, their craft loaded, will ride with the tide and a tail wind up the Mersey tonight as the young couple begin their passage to a new life. The men will not be successful, however. Others will later find rich minerals in the North West.

The lads lined up in c. 1905 with a new plough at the Devonport Carriage Works, the Wheelwright's and Lehman's Blacksmith shop. Colin Dennison Collection.

A grand event in 1902, so they no longer had to go to Latrobe to cross the Mersey, was the opening of the bridge at Devonport.

AN EASY WAY to leave Devonport to resume the Grand Tour is to go from the Bluff south along William Street and turn left to the Bass Highway. You have a wondrous drive ahead towards Launceston, through enchanting villages and productive farmland, thanks to its deep volcanic soil the colour of ochre.

A reliable climate, too, makes the countryside east and west of Devonport a vegetable-growing centre for the nation. You will see the wonders west of Devonport near the completion of our Tour.

Anvers chocolate factory, museum and shop can provide a treat for chocoholics as you near **Latrobe**, 10 km from Devonport. The museum is a former mansion built in 1931. Then turn right at the traffic roundabout beside the Mersey General Hospital and drive to the main street in this fascinating old town by the banks of the Mersey.

It is billed (pardon) the platypus capital of the world. You've got a fair chance of seeing in the wild in the Mersey around here, especially at the Warrawee Forest Reserve upstream, these marsupial freaks with bills like ducks, milk like cows and venom like snakes that lay eggs like chooks. The Visitor Information Centre is in the main street.

The Mersey at Bells Parade, Latrobe, platypus capital of the world.

For its first decades the village grew on this part of the river as the first suitable place from its mouth for a bridge. It was first settled in the mid 1830s, and the town site was laid out and named in 1856 after Charles La Trobe, superintendent of the Port Phillip district, now Victoria. For four months in 1846-7 he was the administrator of Van Diemen's Land. This was after the sacking of a colony governor for licentious conduct (see Naughty Governors, page 134.). The town grew rapidly. The main street, Gilbert Street, is a delight of preserved old shops and other premises, most of them with colonial provenances. Here it is easy to imagine you are back in the 1880s when Latrobe was the largest town on the North West Coast.

From 1870 to 1892 it had three newspapers, a hospital, a brilliant brass band and a lot of taverns for thirsty pioneers. The completion of the railway line from Launceston in 1885 brought a big fillip, moving the hub of the town from near the river east along Gilbert Street to the station. Thousands came from as far away as Hobart for the gala opening on special trains decked in garlands. The England cricket team beat the local gentlemen here in 1888.

Be sure to visit the sublime Bells Parade picnic grounds by the river. W.T. Bell and others built the Mersey's first port here. It flour-ished until the railway's extension to the Mersey heads sealed its fate. It is fittingly the home of the Australian Axeman's Hall of Fame as the first axemen's carnival in the world was held at Latrobe in 1891.

Sherwood Hall next door was built further upstream about 1850 by ex-convict Thomas Johnson and his beautiful part-Aboriginal wife, Dolly Dalrymple. Nineteen years earlier, at Chudleigh near Deloraine, Dolly had saved her children's lives by fighting off a band of Aborigines armed with spears and firebrands who laid siege to her hut for six hours. The relocated and restored Sherwood Hall is well worth a visit.

A gracious icon across the river is Frogmore, a two-storey clas-sical villa with a three-level tower. George Atkinson built it in 1890. More than 600 prints and photographs at the National Trust's Court House Museum (1883) next to the post office will give you a fine visual history of the district.

Back on the Bass Highway, continue east through magnificent undulating farmland at **Sassafras** and beyond. Today it is a patch-work of dark chocolate soil, a variety of crops and green pastures. Only 150 years ago this was dense forest. With only bullock teams and hand tools, it took just three generations to achieve this dramat-ic transformation, effectively completed by 1950. A prominent sign on the left points curiously to Smith and Others Road. The Smith was William, a prominent timber cutter. But others, the Lampreys, nowadays say *they* were the first local settlers.

From here the soil turns from chocolate to grey and travellers going east, as we are, once entered the dense and gloomy Black For-est. This stretch of road, which was unsealed to the 1950s, was the dread of motorists. Before it was formed, horse-drawn vehicles had to bump and slide over saplings laid side by side across the road in swampy areas in winter to prevent them from getting bogged. Early travellers have left nightmarish accounts of the trip through the forest.

A few kilometres further on, you can think of Julius Caesar's fateful advance on Rome in 49 BC when he crossed the Rubicon. Tasmania's Rubicon here is the modest stream you cross, a headwater of the river that enters Bass Strait at Port Sorell. It is just before you reach the old hamlet of **Elizabeth Town.** Its former hotel, now a café bakery, is the only survivor of several stagecoach stopovers between Latrobe and Deloraine. From here you enter a beautiful part of our island settled in the 1830s. Old houses such as Forest Hall, English trees and hedgerows create an idyllic landscape (a legacy

Main street Deloraine, still challenging the forest in 1861. Colin Dennison Collection.

from homesick early settlers) with a backdrop of lofty mountains to the south. Tasmania grows the world's tastiest raspberries. For a superb sampling and other treats visit the Raspberry Farm on our left at Christmas Hills.

Follow the signs a few kms along and leave the Bass Highway for a memorable visit to the picturesque market town of **Deloraine**, first settled about 1823. It has many classified National Trust buildings on each side of the Meander River as it flows from the Great Western Tiers. The local Visitor

Information Centre, on the main concourse, the Emu Bay Road, features Yarns, a large art work in silk of Deloraine's history lovingly worked by local women. The National Trust-run folk museum at the 1856 Family and Commercial Inn is next door. The centre's staff can show you how to get to colonial icons like early flour-mills, the Baptist Tabernacle and Bonney's Inn. The son of a convict, John Bonney opened the inn about 1828. The once-famous wayside establishment, now a fine b & b, retains its thick, panelled walls and cedar mantelpieces. For a while, it was contradictorily called the Temperance Hotel! But, we know, there was a sly sly-grog shop out the back.

Surveyor Thomas Scott named the town after Sir William of Deloraine, of the poem *The Lay of the Last Minstrel* by his kinsman, Sir Walter Scott. The settlement later merged with the older convict settlement of Alveston, over the river, which stubbornly retains its name. The State's first train ran to Deloraine from Launceston in 1871, opening new markets for the district's farmers.

Immediately across the bridge, divert to the right for a few kms to see the magnificent Peppers Calstock, built in the 1830s. It is now a regal b. & b. in manicured parklands. Cedar floors, architraves and furnishings give the residence a warm glow. Even guests' elegant en suite bathrooms are big enough to host a banquet. Calstock's first owner was a former Royal Navy officer, Lieut. Pearson Foote, who ran the place like a ship. His convict servants had to go on parade every morning for the ringing of bells and raising of the Union Jack.

Elegant Peppers Calstock near Deloraine, once run like a battleship and birthplace of Malua, probably the greatest race horse bred in Australia.

It later became a property of the Field family, the early 'cattle kings' of the district who once had a massive 122,000 hectares freehold and leased. It then became a famous horse stud; birthplace of the racing sire Malua, regarded as the greatest all-rounder ever bred in Australia. He won the 1884 Melbourne Cup, the long Adelaide and Geelong cups, plus 5-furlong sprints, and the 3-mile Australian National Hurdle at the grand old age of nine. Malua, incidentally, is Fijian for slow!

The log bridge over the Meander at Deloraine c. 1852. The cottage on the right is Bonney's Inn, still going strong. This is probably the oldest picture of Deloraine. Woodcut from Mrs Meredith's My Home in Tasmania.

SNAPSHOT 1855
Drama on the road to Deloraine

IMAGINE YOU are watching the ducks in a light mist on the Meander across West Parade on a sunny Saturday morning in the winter of 1855. A gang of sullen, chained convicts directed by three redcoats with muskets has just passed by, carting a load of sandstone blocks.

A horn's piercing tarantara bouncing off the river announces the bustling arrival of Ernest Ayton's *Tally Ho!* stagecoach from Launceston. Excited patrons pour from John Bonney's coaching inn behind you and Bonney's new Deloraine Hotel next door as four chestnut and black highsteppers clatter the coach across the timber bridge over the river and turn right towards you. Two farmers selling vegetables and kangaroo carcasses from carts in the street smile in anticipation of boosted business.

Men, women and children about you cheer as the driver in a scarlet jacket stops the dusty black coach. It staggers to and fro for a moment, the steel rims of its wheels crunching the gravel. The odour of sweat wafts from the horses. "You got the mail?" a woman from the hotel asks the coachman.

"Indeed, ma'am!" he replies. "The *royal* mail. And there's tobaccy and rum and the latest papers with the news of the world." It is days since Deloraine has heard about events elsewhere.

"What's left of it, that is," the coachman declares bitterly. "Escaped convicts on horseback bailed us up at gunpoint in the forest five miles out. The scoundrels took some food, a flagon of rum, some money from the gents' pouches as well as their watches. They also nicked one of the lady's brooches and a copy of *The Examiner* and the *Hobarton Mercury* before they rode away, laughing! At least no one was hurt or molested." He leaned down to innkeeper Bonney. "Please summon the troopers, sir."

Two gentlemen in dapper frock coats and tall beaver-skin hats, two ladies in dark crinolines sporting stylish bonnets, two neat young boys in jackets and breeches, a returning farmer in his working attire of brown moleskins and a flannel jacket, his teenage daughter and a smitten-looking young man under a wide-brimmed 'wide awake' hat alight and stretch their limbs after the bumpy journey on scarcely-padded seats.

"Those highwaymen really frightened me," the teenager tells her welcoming mother. "One shoved a pistol in papa's tummy when he swore at them. They could have killed him but they did us no harm."

The two gentlemen tip their hats to the assemblage as they and their lady companions walk up the grassy bank to the hotel for refreshments. The young boy passengers rush into Bonney's Inn. They look as if they are in pain, for it has been a long time since a comfort stop.

Most of the locals follow the mail bag into the inn. The papers will give the news of Victoria's rebellious gold diggers captured at the Eureka Stockade finally being freed, victories by the British and their allies against Russia in the Crimea War. Most interest, though, is the latest news on convict transportation to the island colony officially ending and the name Van Diemen's Land changing to Tasmania; removing the "convict stain" and launching a new era.

The Honey Farm, Chudleigh.

SIDE TRIP
To Chudleigh, Mole Creek and the caves

A REWARDING day trip from Deloraine is to take the B12 bitumen road 27 km through little **Chudleigh** to **Mole Creek** and beyond to the amazing limestone caves in a wooded, hilly landscape honeycombed with caverns and underground streams. This wide and fertile valley is dominated from the south by a rampart of stone, a bulwark of the Central Plateau that is often coated by snow in winter.

Tasmania's distinctive and historic honey industry is on show at The Honey Farm at Chudleigh. It has, with tastings, 50 different types of honey. There is a hive made of glass and a honey industry museum.

The old two-storey brick building on the left as you enter Chudleigh was built as a grain store. In 1853, this and an ale house opposite, Bendemere, were sold to Dan Pickett who set up a hotel and coaching inn. On Saturday evenings, locals congragated there to dance, make merry and play the skittle alley.

Pickett also operated the coach and mail service between Deloraine and Chudleigh until 1890. In the early 1900s the village had four churches, three mixed stores, a post office, railway station, two boot makers, two butchers, one funeral director and hearse, a maternity hospital, a hotel and a one-man police station.

The limestone caves are awesome. We recommend taking a guided Underground Rivers and Glow-worms tour of Marakoopa and/or King Solomons Cave. A popular attraction just east of Mole Creek is the extensive Trowunna Wildlife Park, where you can stroll among all sorts of animals. It is an important refuge for endangered Tasmanian devils. And do see creek-side Wychwood Garden, a treasure specialising in exotic perennials, grasses and shrubs.

The town and the district's name come from the local creek's regular vanishing into the ground then reappearing, like a mole.

Magnificent Wychwood Garden by the trout stream at Mole Creek is a Tasmanian treasure.

FROM DELORAINE, rather than rejoining the Bass Highway, travel east on the old highway over the river to Meander Valley Road, the B54, through the farming centre of **Exton**, to **Westbury.** To your right, as you approach Westbury, is another early Field residence, Westfield, in one of the most imposing settings of any early house in Australia.

We reckon Westbury is the most English of villages in the nation, with English trees lining the streets and hawthorn hedges enclosing nearby fields. Established as a garrison town in 1823, the village had 227 free men and women and 317 convicts. It was planned to become a large market town but, like many other early villages, it failed to meet expectations. There are fine old homes, elegant inns and churches and what is perhaps the only true Village Green in the southern hemisphere.

You will see along the Tour scores of weathered old farm barns like this one east of Deloraine.

Test your navigation skills at the challenging Westbury Maze and Tea Rooms. Pearns Steam World museum's 100 steam engines, mostly from farms, is perhaps the nation's largest collection of the old contraptions.

Continue east on the Meander Valley Road to the old village of **Hagley**. The spire on the left just east of it is on the Anglican Church of St Mary, in a fine old churchyard and built in 1861. It is effectively a monument to the first Tasmanian-born Premier and knight, Sir Richard Dry (1815-69) who gave the land and endowed it. Nearby is Dry's former estate of Quamby. By taking a long carriageway further along the old highway you can visit the imposing early colonial homestead, outbuildings and park.

Taking a break at the Westbury Maze.

Carrick is a further five minutes' drive along the B54 beside the Liffey River, named of course after the stream that passes through Dublin. It was also first settled in 1823. Have a look at the ivy-shrouded Old Mill by the river. The four-level bluestone icon was built in 1846. It operated into the early 1900s, making flour by water-power as Mond's Roller Mills, a reminder of when the Western Plains was a major wheat growing area in the early 19th century. The former Prince of Wales Hotel, now a private residence, dates from 1840. It is three years younger than the convict-built Watch-house across the road. Also in private hands is the 1841 Plough Inn, two storeys of brick, the scene of some rowdy times at old Carrick.

Entally at Hadspen, the 1820s mansion open to the public, the scene of colonial scandal and host to the Duke of Edinburgh.

Spring in the glasshouse at Entally.

OUR TOUR ROUTE turns to the right just beyond Carrick on the B52 road to Longford. But, first, continue 2 km along the Meander Valley Road to the now Launceston dormitory town of **Hadspen**.

Nearby, and our spur for recommending this side-trip, is Entally, an impressive old estate with gardens graced by old oaks. The enterprising Thomas Reibey settled here by the confluence of the South Esk and the Meander rivers in the 1820s. He was the son of a Mary Reibey, who when aged 13 was transported from England for seven years for riding a neighbour's horse without his permission. But Mary prospered in Sydney and is pictured on the Australian $20 note. Thomas Snr's eldest son, Thomas II, was Archdeacon of Launceston from 1857 to 1870. He won a salacious court battle to beat a charge of having his wicked way with the wife of a colleague over a billiards table at Entally. The scandal rocked the colony but did not snooker Thomas' career. He later became Premier of Tasmania.

England's illustrious, bearded cricketer Dr W. G. Grace batted at the ground here when the Colonial gentlemen played England. A guest in 1868 was the Duke of Edinburgh. Gunns Ltd have a vineyard at Entally and manage the property for the Parks and Wildlife Service.

Back west along the Meander Valley Road, turn left to the B52 Illawarra Road and travel through some 10 km of farmland before turning right into graceful old **Longford**, near the confluence of the South Esk and Macquarie rivers. You have now come to the flattest part of the island, with some of its oldest and wealthiest grazing properties.

A drive or stroll up the wide main street, especially at the angular junction of Wellington and Marlborough streets near the Corinthian-columned Municipal Hall, gives you a real flavour of days of yore when settlers created a slice of olde England. An 1897 iron drinking trough for horses with fascinating feet marks the market area in the town centre. Like Westbury, Longford had streets surveyed well into the countryside, with unrealised plans for it to become a large market town.

The settlement here of free farming families forced to move from Norfolk Island in the South Pacific, in 1807 and later, gave the district the name Norfolk Plains. The town became Latour, then Longford after the county in Ireland.

Main Street, Longford, in 2008, looking much as it did in 1850.

Prominent settler Thomas Archer and his three brothers, with convict labour, built the marvellous nearby houses of Brickendon, Woolmers, Panshanger and Northbury while the town, in those thirsty days, grew around the Longford Hotel, built in 1827.

The homestead at Brickendon, Longford.

Christ Church, with an historic graveyard and generous close, is adorned by a bell and clock presented by King George IV. Wellington Street's Georgian Queen's Arms tavern, which we think began dispensing the demon drink as the King's Arms of 1835, is well worth a look. So are the Blenheim Hotel (1846) and the former Make Square Inn, then Tattersalls Hotel (1846), now having a more learned life as the region's library. We recommend the restaurant and accommodation at the old Racecourse Inn at the Marlborough and Bulwer streets corner.

The builder of the first road from Launceston to Longford is reputed to have rendered his bill for the then-princely sum of thirteen pounds. He amazingly agreed, however, to accept instead … a cow! A really rough road, perhaps? Suffered, we suppose, by the travellers on the trusty *Tally Ho!* coach to Launceston from 1833.

Famous painter Tom (Bulldog to his friends) Roberts spent his last years living in his homestead in the district. His grave is in the churchyard at Illawarra, near Longford. Roberts' perhaps most notable work was his 1903 oil *The Opening of the First Parliament of the Commonwealth of Australia.*

Woolmers estate by the Macquarie River, furnished by six generations of Archers.

We like staying in the old cottages at Brickendon Historic Farm and Convict Village a few kms south of the town off Wellington Street. It is still owned by the descendants of pioneer William Archer, now into the seventh generation. The colonial gardens feature the family's Gothic chapel, Dutch barn, workmen's cottages, chicken house, tool and equipment shed and blacksmith's shop. Convicts built all of them. Brickendon and Woolmers (which we will visit soon) are listed on the National Estate register and, as we write, are nominated for World Heritage listing.

Some of the 100,000 blooms at the National Rose Garden, Woolmers Estate.

The grand tour loops south of Longford. Wellington Street becomes Woolmer's Lane, curving left to the Midland Highway.

A highlight along here, just past the Macquarie River, is the fine old Woolmers estate and the National Rose Garden. The estate's homestead, gardens, farm buildings, old cars, photographs, furniture and art are a fascinating collection. Much of the complex enjoys the legacy of the first Thomas Archer who settled here in 1817. Like Brickendon, six generations of his family have lived at Woolmers ever since. They parted with little, preserving a unique sort of time capsule.

If you are here from late spring, through summer to autumn, do not miss the 100,000 or more blooms in the extraordinary and intoxicatingly-fragrant National Rose Garden.

Continue east to the Midland Highway. Turn left here and a few kilometres later turn right for the five km ride to the remarkable historic tourist village of **Evandale**, just south of Launceston Airport. Evandale is a hub of colonial colour, partly from the days when more refined families settled here to eschew the sordid, lawless early years of Launceston. The historic town has a plethora of classified elegant old homes, churches, stores and hotels looking and used as they were when it became a community from 1816.

The town's landmark Water Tower (1896) is on the left in High Street as you drive in. It shows the remains of a grand but failed project to tunnel water to Launceston in the 1830s. Convicts dug the tunnel, mostly about 24 metres deep, for many kms north before the

A street tribute to Evandale's yearly National Penny Farthing Championship.

Evandale's 1896 water tower.

Evandale's Lieut.-Colonel Harry Murray, VC plus, the British Empire's most decorated soldier in World War I, portrayed throwing a grenade.

project was abandoned. Call in at the volunteer-run Visitor Information Centre a block further along for local guidance and a walking-tour brochure.

John, known as Red, the father of bushranger Ned Kelly, was a convict at Evandale before he moved to Victoria. More accomplished celebrities who hailed from the district include the brilliant club-footed painter John Glover, honoured every March by an art prize and exhibition and the subject of a bronze statue in Russell Street, near Falls Park. Other intriguing statues in the street commemorate the town's National Penny Farthing Championship racing on the bicycles in February and also Lieut.-Colonel Harry Murray, VC, CMG, DSO and Bar, DCM, Croix de Guerre. He was the most highly-decorated soldier in the British Empire in World War I. The Tourist Information Centre has a Murray Memorial Room.

Do visit Clarendon Homestead, 10 minutes drive south from Evandale on the C416. It is one of Australia's great houses built in grand proportions. This National Trust treasure has 3.6 hectares of superb parkland with mostly old English trees and shrubs beside the South Esk. An original circle carriageway is in front of the mansion. Convicts built Clarendon for wealthy sheep grazier James Cox about 1838. It is also has a restaurant and a b. & b.

Clarendon, a National Trust treasure south of Evandale, built by the South Esk in 1838.

Sandstone blocks showing in Roman numerals the miles to go to Hobart and Launceston were placed beside the Midland Highway in colonial days. This one is souvenired at Clarendon. Concrete markers replaced them in the 1920s. Then, with Australia's metric conversion in the 1960s, came the kilometre signs of today.

Leaving Evandale, we recommend going to Launceston by turning right off High Street at the Visitor Information Centre into White Hills Road, which becomes Relbia Road. It is another slice of olde England. In November the hedgerows of hawthorn, trees of sloes and plums, and blooming briars present a pageant of fragrant colour. We reckon Everton Lane along here on the right is the most romantic country lane in the nation during spring. The Josef Chromy Vineyard and restaurant are

Refurnished as it was 150 years ago, the National Trust's Franklin House at Youngtown, on our way to Launceston.

at **Relbia**. Your authors gladly confess to a special predilection for its wines and meals, gazing over two trout-laden lakes and grape vines. This is the first of more than a score of vineyards on the Tamar Valley Wine Route, east and west of the Tamar, making brilliant wines. Part 2 of our Tour goes by most of them.

A right turn at the junction with the Old Hobart Road takes you north to the National Trust's beautiful Franklin House on your right beside the Old Hobart Road at **Youngtown** on the outskirts of the city. Rooms in the late Georgian (1838) residence include a ballroom, study, dining room, bedrooms and an original mid 19th-century school classroom looking much as it would have 150 years ago.

Bustling Brisbane Street, Launceston, c 1879. Woodcut from the Australasian Sketcher.

Old Hobart Road will take you north into magnificent **Launceston** (pop. 103,500), teeming with marvellous colonial architecture, parks and gardens. The city has risen from, at times, desperate and downright distasteful days when it was an army-run convict outpost by the Tamar River at the confluence of the North and South Esk from 1805. The Aborigines called it Ponrabbel.

In Prince's Square, the engaging statue of William Pugh, the first to use surgical anaesthetics in the Southern Hemisphere.

The fountain in Prince's Square attracted awe in 1864. Chalmers Presbyterian church is on the right. Woodcut *from* Australia and Tasmania, *Dr. E.G. Robertson.*

Its founder, Lieut. Governor William Paterson, named it, no doubt pleasing his boss, Governor King in Sydney, who hailed from the ancient town of Launceston in Cornwall, England. The River Tamar flows by that city, so guess how this river got its name! Tasmania's early explorers and leaders had a culture of naming places after, or to please, their bosses, starting with Abel Tasman naming the place Van Diemen's Land to honour his boss.

Prisoners labouring on treadmills and others bolted into stocks, gallows with hanged convicts in view and rioting soldiers thirsting for grog once disgraced Launceston streets which today are national examples of splendidly-preserved architectural heritage.

It is Australia's third oldest city (after Sydney and Hobart) and the State's second biggest. Entrepreneur adventurers John Batman and John Pascoe Fawkner sailed from here separately in 1835 to found what is now Melbourne. A remarkable string of community leaders led Launceston's boom years in the mid to late 1800s. Thanks, too, to the mining of gold and tin and the exporting of wheat, wool, grog and food to Victoria's gold fields.

Gracious old Launceston … Doric Greek Revival Milton Hall in front of the Gothic Revival Christ Church and the white-towered former Chalmers Free Church in Frederick Street facing Prince's Square.

Cleric and newspaper editor John West (your authors assert) designed the Australian flag and wrote Tasmania's first book of history, published in 1852. The settlement saw the southern hemisphere's first use of anaesthetics during surgery. It pioneered electric lighting of streets in Australia and was the scene of the nation's first stage play.

It would take the whole book for us to get even near to doing Launceston's heritage justice, so we immodestly commend to you our book *A Walk in Old Launceston*, with a map of the city all of your authors once lived in. The book was published late in 2007 and, like this volume, will be updated regularly.

It is at bookshops, tourist attractions and the Launceston City Council's Travel & Information Centre at the corner of St John and Cimitiere streets. This should be your first stop in the city to get guidance for accommodation and tours and also brochures about the district.

It was a gala day in 1868 when Launceston welcomed Prince Alfred, the colony's first Royal visitor. Prince's Square is on the left. To the right, St Johns.

The Country Club Tasmania resort at Prospect Vale, Launceston. Courtesy the Country Club, Federal Group.

The city is superbly endowed with maintained Georgian, Victorian and Federation period buildings. Our favourite building in Launceston is the mighty Albert Hall in Tamar Street next to City Park. Local artisan John Farmilo built it from 1889 to 1891 for the great Tasmanian International Exhibition to a competition-winning design by local 18-year-old John Duncan. Charles Wooley remembers it as an intimidating place, where he had to sit for school exams. Why can't they build them like that any more?

Must-see places in and around Launceston include the Cataract Gorge where the South Esk tumbles by cliffs and parklands to form the Tamar River, historic City Park and Princes Square, and the outstanding Queen Victoria Museum and Art Gallery.

THIS SECTION has been a big start, with more interesting old towns and cities to see than in any other of the 16 stages of the Grand Tour. So soak up Launceston, Tasmania's Garden City, and enjoy those great old parks before embarking on the wonders of Part 2.

PART TWO 220 km
Launceston, Beaconsfield, George Town, Bridport, Flinders Island

BEFORE LEAVING LAUNCESTON, we note that several Tasmanian airlines can take you to the airport near **Whitemark** on superb **Flinders Island**, where you could spend a separate holiday. Flinders is the major one of more than 50 mostly-uninhabited islands in the Furneaux Group, with 120 pristine beaches.

The islands abound with wildlife. Flinders has good visitor facilities including vehicle hire, wondrous scenery and fishing. Cape Barren Island, a little south of Flinders, has an airstrip and a prospering Aboriginal community, mostly descendants of tribal people sent there from mainland Tasmania in colonial days. At **Wybalenna**, the settlement for exiled Tasmanian Aborigines, an 1830s chapel still stands and the foundations of the huts are visible. The nearby Furneaux Museum at **Emita** demonstrates the stories of Aboriginal heritage, rough and tough early sealers and whalers, the sagas of 65 shipwrecks and has a replica mutton bird processing shed. The Group is the prime home of Cape Barren geese, although some live on the "mainland's" east coast.

The Tamar Valley from near Bradys Lookout. In the foreground, a vineyard protected from predatory birds by netting. Photo, Tony Hope.

SO, OUR TOUR CONTINUES. Cross the Paterson Bridge to join the A7 West Tamar Road along the western shore of the Tamar. Ahead is a recreated Swiss village, a fabulous old gold mining town, seahorses and platypuses, top-notch vineyards selling their products and marvellous towns by the sea, including the fourth and fifth white settlements in Australia.

SNAPSHOT 1847

The tale of the broken-hearted whale

AFTER YOU CROSS the bridge over the Tamar to leave Launceston, imagine that you are sitting on this western shore opposite Royal Park one sunny spring morning on a Sunday in 1847.

You have taken the catamaran-style punt, along with cattle and sheep, over the river from near Ritchie's flour-mill. Two sailing ships carrying cargo are tied up across the water near Soldiers Point (now Home Point) where the North Esk joins the South Esk. A barque there arrived yesterday. You know it is one of the often-bloodied whalers making fortunes for the ships' owners, who sell the mammals' oil for lighting and lubrication.

The sails of the windmill near the semaphore mast on top of Windmill Hill to the east overlooking the settlement are flashing in the sunshine. The Union Jack flutters from the tower of St Johns Church, no doubt with a congregation of gentry, workers and shackled convicts this Sunday.

Suddenly, a tremendous splash in the water nearby shatters your reverie. It's a whale! Its fluked tail smacks the surface as the giant gushes air from its blowhole and dives, heading for the Gorge. A whale! A southern bottlenose, you reckon, going on its glistening brownish skin. Way up here in fresh water; a day's sailing from the coast up a narrow, winding river!

The whale surfaces again as it turns towards the barque. The *whaler*! Men are running about on the deck, waving and yelling. They have seen it. " Thar she blows!" carries across the water. The denizen's nose, you see now, sticks out like the neck of a bottle.

The whale is still rampaging about near the barque 10 minutes later. A crowd of more than 100 people now line the river bank across the water from you. Some are cheering at the spectacle. The commotion has brought them running from church, you suppose.

Three whale-boats leave the shore from near the whaler. Each has six oarsmen. And on the bow the headsman stands, holding his harpoon. The whale charges one boat, tipping its crew into the water. The crowd cheers all the more. The two remaining boats pursue the bottlenose towards the Gorge. A harpoon is thrown, and misses. Blood spurts in the air as another harpoon, from boat three, buries in their quarry.

The spectators roar a mixture of victory and sorrow as the whale charges downstream past you, towing the boat at a mighty pace through water stained red; heading back for the sea, it seems. Some 30 minutes later, as you walk sadly back to the punt, the wounded whale has weakened, a second harpoon has been driven in it, and the dying beast is towed to the barque.

The bottlenose clearly was targetting the whaler. It must have followed the ship from the Bass Strait. Looking for its mate, or its calf, that the whaler took from the sea? Or driven by anguish, seeking bloody revenge?

NOTE: It *might be a coincidence, but Yankee whalers would have spread the tale of the bottlenose when they returned home from Van Diemen's Land. Your authors wonder if it helped inspire American novelist Herman Melville to write the classic* Moby Dick, *about a whale that turned on its hunters. The epic was published in 1851, only four years after the bottlenose visited Launceston.*

***

WEST TAMAR ROAD somehow becomes West Tamar Highway as you pass the suburb of **Riverside**. Countryside with crops, pastures and vineyards slopes to the river. Today the Tamar Valley is an important wine growing region but until the 1950s, after the Huon Valley, it was Australia's second most important apple growing area.

Ferries plied between numerous jetties taking apples to Inspection Head at Beauty Point where they were shipped interstate and overseas.

Although not historic, at **Legana** you can turn left off the highway here on the C732 to visit an enigmatic slice of old rural Switzerland at Grindelwald, built for a nostalgic immigrant from Europe.

Back on the West Tamar Highway turn right to the rocky outcrop you see called Bradys Lookout for a magnificent view of the Tamar Valley. The hill is named after bushranger Matthew Brady, who in the 1820s hung out here to spot potential victims on the

This early tourer stopped his horseless carriage to enjoy the view from the West Tamar. Colin Dennison Collection.

road below to waylay as they journeyed to and from Launceston. An alternative route at Legana is to take the old highway which follows the shoreline at **Rosevears** past many old orchard homesteads, beautiful gardens, vineyards and the historic Rosevears Hotel. From here lovely St. Matthias Church (1843) can be seen across one of the widest reaches of the Tamar. This vista is called **Windermere** because it resembles Lake Windermere in England. Past the Rosevears Hotel a plaque marks the site of the slipyard where John Batman's 30-tonne vessel *Rebecca* was built. He chartered *Rebecca* to take him to Port Phillip.

Stop at the rural-support town of **Exeter** to at least visit its Visitors Information Centre by the highway. It is well stocked with brochures about attractions ahead, west of the Tamar, and can give general guidance. 27 kms on is **Beaconsfield**, the fabulous old gold mining town and the scene of an underground rescue that kept the nation gripped with anxiety for two weeks in 2006.

An alternate, half-hour slower but even prettier way to get there is to turn right a few kms before Beaconsfield towards the river on Gravelly Beach Road, the C728. It hugs the shoreline through **Blackwall** and the village of **Gravelly Beach**, past slipways and moored river craft and vineyards. A splendid BYO cafe there is called Koukla's. It has fine Greek dishes and a river view. The road continues through sublime scenery at **Robigana** and **Deviot**, past the Batman Bridge over the Tamar (which we cross later). Take the B73 Batman Highway back to the West Tamar Highway south of Beaconsfield.

Here was the renowned Tasmania Gold Mine. The Dally brothers in 1877 discovered a huge and fabulously-rich reef of gold near today's mine. Prospectors swarmed in and the town grew rapidly and boisterously, as mining towns do. It fuelled northern Tasmania's late 19th century boom years and made some Launceston families rich. A steam train ran from the town to its port at Beauty Point.

The head of the gold mine at Beaconsfield. Photo, Tony Hope.

An old workhouse, a steam tractor, pensioned off at Beaconsfield. Photo, Tony Hope

When flooding eventually made the mine unworkable in 1914 with pumping equipment of the day, 836,556 ounces of gold had been produced. Modern de-watering equipment enabled the mine's reopening and the first gold ingot of the new era was poured in 1999.

The West Tamar Council's Beaconsfield Mine and Heritage Centre in the mine's former pump houses has an excellent display of the town's and the mine's glory days.

There is also a reconstructed crushed cage in which miners Brant Webb and Todd Russell were trapped for fourteen days a kilometre underground in 2006.

Beauty Point is a casual few minutes drive north of Beaconsfield on the A7 West Tamar Highway, which goes by the Port Dalrymple Yacht Club, the Australian Maritime College (the nation's premier teacher of mariners) and the Tamar Yacht Club. A little farther on, the once busy Inspection Head apple shipping wharves are now home to two popular attractions for visitors: Seahorse World and Platypus House.

Another 17 km north on the A7 takes you to the western mouth of the Tamar at the holiday retreat of **Greens Beach**, near West Head. But on the way have a good look at remains of **Yorktown**. A monument marks this as the first seat of government in the colony's north in December 1804. This was soon after the first settlers, who had gone to Outer Cove where George Town is today, moved across the river to these supposedly greener pastures. They left a few people behind at what became an outpost.

The party had sailed from Sydney Harbour in four boats on 15 October 1804 led by Scots Lieut. Governor William Paterson. There were 67 soldiers, a doctor, 74 convicts and two convicts' wives, 20 other women, 14 children and a solitary free settler farmer. They were farewelled by a military band and an 11-gun salute. Clearing and construction began at what Paterson then called York Town, later Yorkton, in December. 30 to 40 buildings were erected including a cottage grandly called Government House. Paterson described the settlement as having "a very pretty appearance". Pioneer explorers Matthew Flinders and George Bass named the general Tamar region Port Dalrymple after eminent Scots hydrographer Alexander Dalrymple. When the boats left, about 205 people including convicts remained at York Town. Letters between Paterson and governors in Sydney referred to this as the site for the future capital of the north.

But Sydney-based Governor Lachlan Macquarie came here with his wife and a big party in 1811 to stay at Government House. Evidently he detested the place. His journal records it as having no inhabitants apart from the guard and the government gardener. "A deserted, desolate village", Macquarie wrote of this bonny place, among other insults. It seems he did not like Launceston, either, as you will read when we get to George Town.

The West Tamar Historical Society and Victoria's La Trobe University in 2006 conducted archaeological digs at the site. They unearthed brick foundations and wall plaster from Paterson's Government House along with crockery and a plate. The York Town Vineyard, incidentally, grows splendid pinot noir and pinot gris on a hill of gravel.

The ubiquitous Governor Macquarie, who moved the northern capital north to George Town.

Governor Paterson

Elizabeth (nee Campbell) Macquarie, immortalised by scores of places her husband named after her.

Take the A7 highway back to Beaconsfield. Turn left into Grubb Street, which becomes Auburn Road for a memorable trip through wine and cattle country. Your authors have a special liking for wines at the Holm Oak Vineyards on West Bay Road, off the C724 Rowella Road on the left at **Rowella**. Continue south beside the Tamar on Rowella Road. Then keep by the river at **Sidmouth**, taking Auld Kirk Road where you can see the 1843 Auld Presbyterian Kirk. Continue to Deviot and the Batman Bridge, on which we cross the river.

Turn left on the A8 East Tamar Highway for a 30 km run past some big industrial centres and the busy port of Bell Bay to thriving and historic **George Town**. The Visitor Information Centre is on the corner of Main Road and Victoria Street. This is the nation's oldest continuously-settled town, excluding Sydney and Hobart, that grew into cities.

Locals claim it is also the third site of white settlement in Australia, after Sydney and Hobart. Locals across the river at Yorktown make the same claim. They all disregard, though, the 1788 settlement from Sydney at Norfolk Island, which is part of Australia. So, if you are fussy, George Town rates No. 4 and Yorktown No. 5. But what a history George Town has!

An obelisk marks the spot at now-York Cove where a ceremony on 11 November 1804 marked settlement six days after the whites arrived. Looking on from bushes were bemused Aborigines whose ancestors had lived on this island for 40,000 years. But after a couple of months Colonel Paterson decided the land was not suitable and moved his party across the river to then-York Town, which we tourers have visited. But George Town later struck back.

Late in 1811, years after Paterson cleared off to Launceston, then left the colony, Sydney's Governor Macquarie, the profligate namer of places after himself and his wife, visited Launceston, and then York Town. As your authors noted earlier, the governor did not like either place. He crossed the river from York Town and found this spot, called Outer Cove, pleasing. He had it surveyed and sent a despatch from his tent to Launceston, commanding that the admin-

Colonial George Town c. 1857. Woodcut by J. Cooper after Bishop Nixon. Old Tasmania Prints, *Clifford Craig.*

istration of the north of the colony and its military and convict trappings be sent back down the river to the place he then called George Town after King George III, the sovereign of the day. He dubbed the inlet here York Cove and the tiny stream running into it York River (now York Rivulet) after the Duke of York. Macquarie had two boards marked George Town nailed to trees. He then boarded *Lady Nelson*, which had brought the first European settlers here, and sailed home to Sydney without facing the good folk of the doomed capital up the river.

Many settlers were reluctant to move from Launceston on Macquarie's orders but the relocation became official in 1819. George Town was still the capital two years later when Governor Macquarie returned. He records that even the convicts cheered his arrival.

Still well pleased, we assume, he named streets as they are today. They are just about a Who's Who of the colony and the British Empire about then. The two main streets are, of course, Macquarie and Elizabeth, not after a queen but Macquarie's wife. Other streets honour queens Victoria, Adelaide and Anne plus King William. Then come British notables and politicians Wellington, Bathurst and Goulburn. V.D.L. and N.S.W. governors and commandants are honoured by Paterson, Arthur, Cimitiere, Franklin and Sorell streets. Then he signed warrants for the hanging of nine convicts.

The esteemed visitor's disdain for Launceston has resulted in it being the only notable old town in Australia without a Macquarie Street. Place names authority Wayne Smith has counted 99 places in Tasmania named after Macquarie, his wife and his chums. Macquarie's journals from his visits to the island in 1811 and 1821 reveal him bestowing appellations on 20 and more locations in a day. Mercifully, some names have since been changed. More about that at several more places on our Tour.

The north's headquarters returned to Launceston in 1825 on orders from London. Thereafter for 150 years George Town experienced a little growth with gold mining but slumbered as a small village and later a holidaying place until its reawakening with the opening upstream of Comalco Aluminium in 1955 and the ferro-alloy processor Temco in 1962. A sad price of this progress was the destruction of many old buildings.

Young Hobart mariner Captain James Kelly sailed into town for a remarkable visit in 1816. He was continuing his voyage around the island we write about along the Tour at Strahan. Kelly and his crew of four oarsmen with a tiny sail on their whaleboat were a ragged-looking lot. They were confederates of the rampaging bushranger Michael Howe, George Town's commandant decided.

The protesting five were smartly arrested, chained and bundled into cells. That evening, however, Kelly was able to convince said commandant that they had once dined together in Hobart; that Kelly had been despatched by his friend, the governor. A humbled commandant that night hosted a slap-up banquet for his former captives. But 18 months later a bushranger named Geary and his gang raided the town, trussed up the soldiers, released six convicts to join his gang and sailed off in two stolen boats laden with grog.

The Huon pine replica of the sloop Norfolk, in which Bass and Flinders sailed around Van Diemen's Land in 1798 to prove it was an island. She is sailing off The Nut at Stanley in a re-enactment of that voyage in 1998 by Bern Cuthbertson and crew. The replica is in George Town's Bass and Flinders Centre.

A replica of James Kelly's boat *Elizabeth* is part of the display at the Bass and Flinders Centre. It is opposite the 1856 Pier Hotel in Elizabeth Street. The centre also has a wondrous Huon pine replica of *Norfolk*, the sloop Bass and flinders sailed in 1798 to where George Town is now when circumnavigating Van Diemen's Land to prove it was an island. The centre's nautical displays include 15 well-travelled quilts titled collectively What Bass and Flinders Saw.

On his way from Launceston to found what became Melbourne in 1835, wicked John Batman supposedly planned his trip over a pint or five at the Steam Packet Inn, licensed four years later in 1839, next to the future site of

The Grove, the gracious home of Port Officer and George Town Magistrate Matthew Friend RN from 1835. It and its restaurant are often open to the public.

the centre. The former inn is now Whitestones, a private residence. Batman traded clothes, food and tools with Aboriginal chiefs for about 240,000 hectares of land at Port Phillip. He bragged that he was "the largest landowner in the world" but the government later cancelled the dodgy deal.

Old buildings around George Town include the 1830s Tara Hall in Sorell Street, probably the town's oldest standing building; the 1855 Watch House Museum in Macquarie Street, which is loaded with memorabilia; and the 1846 George Town Hotel, once the British Hotel. The Grove (1830s), the town's best-known old building, opens to the public on Thursdays.

Take the A8 Low Head Road for a 10-minute drive north of George Town near the river to sublime **Low Head**, which abounds with history and became a popular holiday spot in the early 1900s. Half way to Low Head is Marion Villa, built in 1835 as the holiday retreat of wealthy James Cox, owner of Clarendon, near Evandale. Further on are the two picturesque c.1881 stone lighthouses, called the leading lights, with their former keepers' houses.

Low Head's first stone lighthouse, which operated for 57 years from 1833. Woodcut by J. Cooper after Bishop Nixon 1857. Black & White Photographics.

Today's distinctive Low Head light.

The Pilot Station here was established in 1805, the year the English won the Battle of Trafalgar. It is the oldest continually-used one in Australia. Pilots are still needed for some ships to navigate the dangerous entrance. The oldest surviving buildings here go back to 1834 and it is arguably the most intact and significant early maritime precinct in Australia. Its Maritime Museum has 12 rooms of displays.

Towards the lighthouse on the left is the original cable station headquarters built c. 1859 to service the first underwater telegraph cable across Bass Strait. Here you can go on a short penguin rookery walk by the shore, where fairy penguins nest overnight.

From 1805, when a ship was sighted as the sun was setting, a fire was lit at the site of today's lighthouse and kept blazing all night to keep the vessel in touch with the port. The light station was established 28 years after the signal station to guide ships at the narrow, reef-ridden and tidal mouth of the Tamar. The first stone lighthouse was built in 1833 and replaced by the present brick one in 1890. More than 12 ships were wrecked here until the early 1900s.

Today's lighthouse has the only diaphone fog-horn still in working order in the nation. It operated from 1929 to 1973 and then became neglected and forgotten, but enthusiasts have restored it as a tourist attraction. Its deafening warning could be heard 10 kms away.

From 1830, shipping arrivals and other news was sent in minutes by semaphore from Low Head, Mount George and Mount Direction to Windmill Hill in Launceston. The arrival of the electric telegraph made this system obsolete. You can see a replica on the rise below the lighthouse and another with a 360-degree view is on Mount George, east of George Town.

Young Charlie Wooley and his schoolmates used to catch crayfish from the rocks below the lighthouse, sort of snagging the crustaceans in the boys' mums' old stockings. "But we just threw them back," Charles recalls. "Amazingly, we didn't know they were good to eat!" Young Peter Mercer looked for a catch in stone colonial fish traps and sampled abalone that were abundant there. Michael Tatlow swam at Low Head surf carnivals.

Return to George Town. About 5 km south on the East Tamar Highway, turn left to join the B82 road for a 55 km ride of wonders through bush and farming land. Visit the old gold mining ghost town of **Lefroy** and the remains of its once famous Pinafore Lode. Brilliant wines are on sale at vineyard restaurants past **Pipers River** on the way to the favourite old fishing port and beach-side holiday resort of **Bridport,** the sea cargo gateway to Flinders Island.

Bands of the north-east Aboriginal tribe had lived around here for millennia when rough sealers came from the Furneaux islands in the early 1800s to capture tribal women as wives and to kill seals for them. Surveyor Thomas Lewis, who did most of his work from a craft off the coast, came from Dorset, England. The municipality retains the name he gave the district, Dorset. Bridport and at least six other place names around here have the same origin.

The first settlers came to Bridport in 1832. Surveyed in 1859 and proclaimed a township in 1883, it grew slowly as a farming and shipping centre. Finds of gold and tin livened things for a while but the new Launceston to Scottsdale railway line took over Bridport's minerals export business.

The town today is a prosperous retirement, fishing and holiday spot of about 1,400 residents, with good accommodation options and a caravan park. An early settled farm east of the town now has the Barnbougle Dunes links golf course, ranked the No.1 public-access course in Australia and one of the best 50 in the world.

Vines galore in the sweeping countryside at Pipers Brook on the Tamar Valley Wine Route. Photo Tony Hope.

PART THREE 165 km
Scottsdale, Derby, Weldborough, St Helens

THERE ARE SCORES of villages and attractions in the North East that would require weeks to explore. Our Tour goes to many of them. From Bridport, take the B84 Bridport Road through 24 km of forest and farmland to **Scottsdale**.

Before entering the town of 2,000 residents, we sightseers who want to make the most of this precious part of the world should heed a sign on the right inviting you to visit the Bridestowe Lavender Estate, 23 km away off the B81 at little Nabowla. It is the southern hemisphere's largest and oldest farm of true lavender, grown originally from seeds imported from France in 1920. During peak flowering in December through to February, the aroma will tingle your nostrils before you see a 50-hectare purple blaze of flowers. It produces about 800 litres of precious lavender oil a year. There is also a visitor centre, souvenir shop and café. You will leave there a fragrant traveller. Bridestowe is closed at weekends in winter.

Greeting you with a burst of colourful fragrance, the Bridestowe Lavender Estate at Nabowla, west of Scottsdale.

For information about the North East Trail, go to Scottsdale's Forest EcoCentre and Visitor Information Centre in a wondrous building in King Street that looks to us like a giant space capsule. A covered walkway around the circular construction has exhibits about the fertile district's history. Attractions you can be directed to include Forestry Tasmania's Hollybank Treetops Adventure, 15 minutes' drive away. Experiences here include gliding in a harness attached to wires through the treetops above Pipers River.

The site of Scottsdale first copped a few names including Cox's Creek and Cox's Paradise (after a pioneer called Cox who bragged a lot about his patch) and Heazlewood when the coastal plains were farmed from the 1830s. Then came Scotts New Country after surveyor James Scott, who led six men on a tough surveying trek to the North East in the early 1850s. He opened up heavily-forested lands of chocolate soil for hardy pioneers to select.

Scottsdale was officially named in 1893, soon after the coming

of the all-important railway from Launceston. Notable historic buildings in town include the 1890s-built National Trust classified Anabel's of Scottsdale, now a restaurant, and the 1880s Old Post Office, now the town's splendid folk museum.

Looking like a landed spacecraft, the innovative Forest Eco and Visitor Info. centres, with colourful displays, King Street, Scottsdale.

From Scottsdale, continue on the A3 Ringarooma Road, which becomes the Tasman Highway. The North East Trail you have been on becomes the Trail of the Tin Dragon as you get to the old tin mining towns of **Branxholm**, then **Derby** and later **Moorina** and **Weldborough**. They are in exquisite farming and forest country with lush valleys and gurgling streams where European explorers first found and mined some gold and then tin all over the place from the early 1870s. There were already a score of little tin mines in the district when about 1,000 Chinese fossickers arrived by sea through Bridport and St Helens from the late 1870s. In the cemetery at Moorina are Chinese graves, an altar and stove where food was cooked and left for the departed.

Times were tough for the pioneer settlers in the 1800s.

They were hard working and frugal men, who trotted about usually in single file, pigtails swinging at their shoulders, their provisions and the minerals they found packed in baskets on bamboo poles bending from their shoulders. The wives of a few of them also came and opened small retail stores. A Joss House temple from Weldborough is displayed at the Queen Victoria Museum in Launceston. It is one of the few remaining complete relics of the Chinese presence from this fascinating phase in Tasmanian history.

A visitor reading the news to a Chinese tin miner at his rickety slab home near Mount South Cameron, north of Derby, in 1903. Weekly Courier newspaper.

A Chinese motif at the scene of the 1877 Battle of Branxholm Bridge, when white miners confronted the Chinese. Created by A.S. & D.M. Edwards, Geoff, Ivo & Frank.

Monuments to Chinese tin miners are common at old bushland cemeteries along the Trail of the Tin Dragon.

*Harvest time in the lush meadows of the North East in the late
1800s. Black & White Photographics.*

But they attracted some racist resentment from white miners,
who reckoned "the Celestials" were taking their tin and gold and
employment. The white miners around Branxholm in 1877 heard
that 12 new Chinese miners were walking in from Bridport. We
have from old-time white miner Tas Kincaide the story of how the
whites, liquored up and armed with guns and forks, confronted the
Chinese at the bridge over the Ringarooma River at Branxholm. The
Chinese quailed before the abuse and threats of death. They retreated until police from Scottsdale and Launceston cleared their passage. The confrontation is remembered as the Battle of Branxholm
Bridge, noted by rows of coloured Chinese motifs on the walls of the
new bridge in Branxholm. The new Tin Centre at Derby relates and
illustrates the district's colourful mining past.

The Chinese, who also panned sapphires, used ancient engineering skills to construct long channels of water for sluicing minerals. They ran their canals through massive rocks by drilling holes
in them and driving sticks in the holes. Water then poured on the
sticks made them swell, splitting the rocks. By 1882 Chinese miners
at scores of sites outnumbered the whites. Law-abiding hard workers and all, the Chinese were irrepressible gamblers. Seven of them
around here were travelling agents for a sort of numbers-game lot-

tery called "white pigeon". And, your authors have discovered, we were wrong in thinking, as is the official story, that Wrest Point in Hobart was Australia's first legal casino. The hardy Chinese of the North East had a few of them in the last couple of decades of the 1800s. A big ripper gambling house was in Weldborough. A hundred or more played fan tan and a sort of roulette there every night behind a complex of doors with armed guards. European and Chinese gamblers flocked to Weldborough from all parts of Australia.

The mining boom ended about 1910 but a few individual fossickers still extract tin from "them thar hills". Many Chinese remained in Tasmania, though. Their descendants include business and political leaders and a couple of pretty good cricketers, David Boon and Ricky Ponting.

Derby's circa 1888 Bank House is a National Trust classified property, the oldest remaining timber bank building in Tasmania. It closed in 1991. Bank House has a fine range of antiques and craft goods.

From near **Herrick** is an interesting possible long side-trip north on the B82 through **Pioneer**, past Blue Lake, a former open-cut mine, and **Gladstone** to the Eddystone Point historic lighthouse of granite. Then go south inland on the C843 to St Helens. But by going this way you miss many splendours.

Back on the Trail of the Tin Dragon past Weldborough, you drive through forests of wattles ablaze with flowers of gold in early spring. The Weldborough Pass Scenic Reserve has one of the best stands of myrtle trees in the State. The road descends to the sublime **Pyengana** valley where you can sample its famous cheeses and visit the village's old Pub in the Paddock. Further east in the scrub left and right, many early tin mining diggings that can still be seen.

At **St Helens**, by lovely and sheltered Georges Bay, you enter Tasmania's East Coast microclimate. It is generally warmer and drier here because a tropical ocean current flows south near the coast, which is also usually free of the cold prevailing winds that belt the west, south and the Highlands. The warm water attracts tuna and

The glorious East Coast ... a sea of indigo-and-sky-blue lapping beaches of glistening white at Binalong Bay, north of St Helens.

marlin that provide big-game fishing. A yearly highlight is the St Helens Game Fishing Classic, in March. The presence of pelicans along the East Coast at any time of year confirms that this is a warm place.

With a population of about 2,000 rising to 15,000 in summer holidays, it is the east coast's largest town, fuelled largely by tourism and fishing. British Captain Tobias Furneaux sailed up the coast in 1773 and named St Helens Point at the southern end of Georges Bay in memory of a place on Britain's Isle of Wight. Whalers and sealers were regular visitors in the early 1800s. Coastal land grants were made to European settlers from 1830. The finding of tin inland at Blue Tier in 1874 and a rush of mostly Chinese miners made St Helens a booming export centre for a while. The district's past is well presented at the St Helens History Room in the Visitor In-formation Centre off Cecilia Street. Exhibits include items left by Aborigines, Chinese and colonial ship builders. There is a beautifully-constructed working model of the huge Anchor Mine water-wheel and massive ore-crushing hammers called stampers. Also a model of the long-gone mountain-top town of Poimena at nearby Blue Tier, which is worth driving to. Sadly, many of St Helens' heritage buildings have been modernised or destroyed but an avenue of elms planted in 1890 is a feature of the town.

Beer-barrel Beach around here got its name from the day a flotilla of beer barrels washed up there from a wrecked ship. The excitement of locals who rushed to the beach, we understand, evaporated when they found that the barrels were empty. The town has two caravan parks and good places to dine and stay. It is a splendid spot to spend time on long, glistening-white beaches lapped by remarkably clear water or going on nature walks. We wonder how Swim-cart Beach got its name.

There is fine rock and surf fishing at the little resort town of **Binalong Bay**, 11 km north-east on the C850. Humbug Point here is in memory of local farmer and Government surveyor J. H. Wedge, who it seems bah humbugged a lot to people who challenged his claims that Tasmanian tigers, or thylacines, had attacked his sheep, often found dead in his paddocks. Tigers did live around here,

The Tasmanian Tiger, once the target of bounty hunters. Litho by Harriet Scott, 1871. From Krefft's Mammals of Australia.

though. Some might still live in the wild but the official last of them died at a zoo in Hobart in 1936. Their end was hastened by a government bounty placed on their heads because of, probably exaggerated, fears the carnivore marsupials preyed on sheep. Aboriginal cave paintings 20,000 years old and archeological finds show that thylacines once ranged throughout Australia, especially in tropical Arnhem Land.

Rocks splashed red and orange by lichen meet the greenery at the Bay of Fires. Photo by Garry Richardson, Wanderer Photographics, St Helens.

A little farther north is the magnificent Bay of Fires conservation area, named by the same Captain Furneaux who, from his ship, saw smoke from fires at Aborigines' campsites. The bay has scores of Aboriginal middens of oyster, scallop and abalone shells.

Big boulders of granite splashed with bright red and orange lichen punctuate the coastline and more beaches fair glitter in the sun. Divers come to the Bay of Fires to explore luxuriant forests of kelp and submerged caves. The bay, but not the road, extends many kms north to the Eddystone Point lighthouse, which was a blessing to Michael Tatlow one dark night before the coming of GPS gear when he nearly lost his bearings sailing up the coast to Flinders Island in the wake of colonial sealers and explorers.

Also extinct, the little Tasmanian emu, common when whites settled in Van Diemen's Land. This is the only-known live picture of the bird, regularly hunted by colonials. Etching from Latham's General History of Birds c. 1828.

PART FOUR 85 km
St Marys, Bicheno, Coles Bay
Plus a side trip to Cornwall, Fingal, Mangana and Mathinna

THE TASMAN HIGHWAY south from St Helens follows the coast much of the way for 20 km through little **Beaumaris** to the holiday and beachside fishing village of **Scamander**.

You could take the shorter coast road through pretty **Falmouth** but, to soak up some fascinating mining history and old pioneering villages, we recommend continuing on the A3 for 8 kms up steep St Marys Pass. In places here you can look down from the road to the tops of big gum trees only metres away. Convicts kept at a probation station near Falmouth and at the top (but oddly called Grassy Bottom) must have had a devil of a time building the pass in the mid 1840s so inland farmers could get themselves and their produce to the sea.

The old St. Marys railway station, once the end of the line, now a fine restaurant.

St Marys is a farming town at the head of the early-settled Fingal Valley nestling just west of a dominating pyramid-like mountain called St Patricks Head. British Captain Furneaux, mentioned at St Helens, named it 30 years before white settlement on the island.

He had lost touch with Captain James Cook in HMS *Endeavour* and was sailing past in HMS *Adventure* en route to New Zealand.

The name St Patrick just might have enticed several Irish pioneers to come here. One of them had the town called Armagh for a while until he returned to Ireland. The town faced the comical prospect of being called Grassy Bottom but a tut tutting grazier had the name obliterated. The barely-settled spot was proclaimed St Marys under the Waste Lands Act (!) in 1857. One of the first buildings was a grog shop on the site of today's St Marys Hotel. Thirst came first all over old Tasmania.

The upper valley's Irish heritage is indicated nearby by the hamlets of **Dublin Town** and **Irishtown**, sometimes confused with little Irishtown in the far northwest. There is also a **German Town**. St Marys has an

The school drum and fife band, St Marys in 1920.

historic railway station, with a display of colonial photographs.

The town has changed little since Michael Tatlow commuted to school here from Fingal, farther down the valley, decades ago. Also long ago, young visitor Charlie Wooley peered over the side of the little bridge crossing St Marys Rivulet in the main street. "I was capti-

The opening of the Fingal Valley's first coal mine at Cornwall, west of St Marys, in 1886. Photo courtesy Jim Haas.

vated, dazzled by this first sight of trout which were flashing about," he recalls. "They were looking at me." His captivation became a passion for fly-fishing for trout that has not diminished.

SIDE TRIP   *Bare Rock, the stained sentinel south of Fingal.*

Cornwall, Fingal, Mangana and Mathinna

YOU CAN SPEND a rewarding day or two from St Marys in brilliant river valleys and old coal and gold mining villages in the Break O Day and South Esk river valleys.

10 minutes' drive west on the A4 Esk Main Road on your right is the short road to the Mt Nicholas Range and the colourful old coal mining town of **Cornwall**, named after the mining county in England.

Mega millions of tonnes of coal were won with pick and shovel in the early years from mines tunnelled and shafted into seams in the hills. Miners stained black by coal dust and with carbide-powered lights on their helmets lugged skips of their "black gold" by hand and pit ponies to fuel Tasmanian industry. Michael Tatlow, then aged nine, spent a day in the Black Cat mine near Fingal and came our with his face and arms as black as, well, coal. Four mines still operate in the district.

Former miner and local historian Jim Haas helps run the Cornwall Coalminers Heritage Wall, with the names of some 1,200 men who worked the mines here. Visitors are encouraged to take the Coalmine Heritage Walk around the town and to a couple of disused mines.

33 km on west from Cornwall along the A4 through sheep and cattle country, going over the meandering little Break O Day river, you could stay at the intriguing old mining and pastoral town of **Fingal** (pop. 600). A huge, slabby cliff called Bare Rock presides over the town from the south. A mine in hills to the left of Bare Rock still yields coal. It is railed from the end of the line near the town, which holds the World Coal Shovelling Championship every March.

Fingal's wide main street of old buildings is easily passed through by travellers unaware of the centre's rich heritage and sublime countryside. Fine examples of sandstone stables confront you in the car park behind the Fingal Hotel, built by convicts. A dog kennel is built into a sandstone stairway behind the pub. It is next to the former entrance to the inn's storehouse of precious grog. A mastiff chained to the kennel countered larcenous attempts by thirsty colonial miners and farm hands. Staff will gladly show off the hotel's cellar. But we warn you that the former dungeon for troublesome convicts is now the abode of Patrick, the ghost of one of them. Michael Tatlow lived at the hotel for a few years as a lad when his family owned it.

The colourful former stables built by convicts at the back of the Fingal Hotel. Below the stone steps is a kennel for a mastiff to terrify colonial intruders near the hotel's liquor store to its right.

The South Esk, flowing in a huge arc from Mathinna via Fingal and Evandale to Launceston. And sublime enough for sometimes-troutless Tatlow and Wooley to claim we go there for the scenery. Photo Charles Wooley.

Going for it at Fingal's yearly World Coal Shovelling Championship at the footy ground.

He and Charles Wooley take hopeful mates to Fingal now and then to cast flies to the amusement of the South Esk's trout. Some fine but wily denizens lurk in a broad-water of the river a few hundred metres from the pub. The town also has a couple of fine b. & bs.

Your authors think it was Irish settler James Grant who named Fingal in 1821 after the town that now hosts Dublin International Airport. But many such origins are disputed in Tasmania. Some records credit land commissioner Roderick O'Connor, when the village got a convict station about 1824.

Gracious Malahide Estate c. 1845. The lord of the manor, The Hon. William Talbot, setting out for Fingal, virtually a hamlet to serve the estate. Tinted lithograph by Royston & Brown, 1845. From Old Tasmanian Prints *by Clifford Craig.*

The hotel was once the St Andrews Inn, then the Talbot Arms. The wide main street is Talbot Street, after William Talbot from Ireland. He was granted land and convict workers in 1824 to create and run a farming estate near the village at the confluence of the Break O Day and the South Esk. It is named Malahide, after the Talbot family castle in eastern Ireland. The village for a while was virtually a place in the style of feudal England; there to support the lord in his manor. Like many early towns, Fingal was surveyed to be a metropolis in the mid 1800s. It has about 50 km of wide back streets around pretty empty blocks.

The Aboriginal name for the South Esk was Mangana Lienta. Thus little old **Mangana**, about 10 kms away across the river. It was The Nook when hundreds of men and women toting picks and pans scurried to the place in 1852 as the news spread that gold had been

Welcome to Mangana. A once-cosy home, ravaged by the years. The village, however, has some nicely-restored buildings.

found there. This was the first gold strike in Van Diemen's Land. The Nook's fossickers had little luck, though. The hamlet still has several maintained old buildings but also a lot that are overgrown and rotting.

Deer still roam in Tasmania's forests.

Steep Pepper Hill road will take you from Mangana to the former mining towns of **Rossarden** and **Storeys Creek** on the southern slopes of towering Ben Lomond. Chinese prospectors found rich lodes of tin and wolfram there in the 1870s. Their small claims were amalgamated into mechanised mines that became the major producers of tin in the nation. But by 1982 the ore was mostly gone and the mines closed. Charles Wooley remembers Rossarden as a raw and isolated place, where he sometimes trudged through snow armed with a pocket of stones to fight his way to Sunday school against local young toughs. His father ran the mine's power station. Rossarden is recovering from its ghost town days as a tourism centre and even has a first-rate golf course.

The lucky gold scratchers were those who left Mangana and went up the valley to **Mathinna**, half an hour's drive north from Fingal on the B43 Mathinna Road by the captivating upper reaches of the South Esk.

The fabulous Black Boy and Golden Gate mines at Mathinna were touted as the richest gold mines in the world for a while. The town boomed in the late 1800s when the Golden Gate mine, for instance, employed 300 men a shift. There were about 20 official and sly grog shops, at least three football teams and gambling dens for

Shopping at Abbott's General Store, Mathinna, in 1904. The gold mine was over the hill at the back.

The Union Jack fluttering over the New Golden Gate mine at Mathinna in 1896, one of the richest the world has seen.

the Chinese fossickers. Many 19th century buildings, mostly timber ones, still line the main street. Some alluvial gold is found near the town from time to time and exploration continues. As with many old mining towns, the next bonanza is coming. There's more of it still in the ground, locals say, than was ever taken.

The town is named after a pretty Aboriginal girl who never went there. Toddler Mathinna was adopted at Government House in Hobart by Lieut. Governor Sir John Franklin and his wife Lady Jane. The girl was a sparkling presence there. But when the Franklins returned to England she was dumped in an orphanage. Mathinna fretted; torn between the worlds of her tribal parents and of her adoption, and accepted by neither. She was still a young woman when her body was found in a stream. Mathinna had drowned while drunk. Ballet dancer Graeme Murphy, father of the Sydney Dance Company, grew up in Mathinna.

See some interesting old photographs and meet the locals at the grandly-titled Mathinna Country Club. Nearby Mathinna Falls Reserve walk goes through a spectacular rain forest to a mighty waterfall after rain. Evercreech Forest Reserve has the stately White Knights, the world's tallest ghost gums. And good camping facilities are at the Griffin Forest Reserve, 5 km from Mathinna.

RETURN TO ST MARYS, if you have taken the Fingal Valley trip, for a 45 km roller-coaster ride down Elephant Pass and along the coast to **Bicheno**.

Turn south at the St Marys Hotel into Story Street, which becomes Gray Road, which irritatingly becomes the A4 Elephant Pass Road in this State where so many thoroughfares change names without much, often no, signage to enlighten navigating visitors. To further confuse, at the coast by Chain of Lagoons, our A3 Tasman Highway is joined by the other Tasman Highway that passes through Falmouth. But, brave tourer, your authors know the way.

Logging in the days before chain saws and clear felling. Photo, courtesy Bev. and Kevin Short.

Elephant Pass is named from Mt Elephant which, from the road to St Marys from Fingal, looks a bit like the profile of an elephant. Take a tasty break in bushland at Mt Elephant Pancakes. Photographers can capture a host of marvellous seascapes, then landscapes at the Douglas Apsley National Park, on the way to **Bicheno**.

Some of the most enthralling hours of our Tour are waiting 22 km from Chain of Lagoons and 7 km north of Bicheno at East Coast Natureworld. We rate it the outstanding natural wildlife and ecology park in the nation, complete with a recreated colonial coal mine. Bruce and Maureen Englefield have developed 65-hectares of bush, parklands and coastal lagoons where you can stroll among all sorts of animals including forester kangaroos, fallow deer and wombats. Even Tasmanian Devils and deadly snakes look at home in large compounds. At one exhibit showing off labelled, dried droppings from different critters you will see that wombat dung is cubed! The Englefields, aged 65, ran in the 2008 London Marathon to raise money to help save the devil from a potentially-extincting disease.

They gave part of Natureworld to the State Government for a big Devil Island home for disease-free devils, contributing to Bruce Englefield being named Tasmanian of the Year in 2008 for his devil-saving works. Thanks, mate. Sales of this book will help to fund Devil's Island.

The Tassie Devil that greeted us at wondrous Natureworld, north of Bicheno. The reserve has a unique Devil Island to help save the threatened species.

A highlight is Natureworld's unique nocturnal house. Night-active animals you rarely see in the wild live naturally here in an environment with a computerised 12-hour time delay. For instance, of a morning they think it is yesterday's sunset, along with sounds recorded in the nearby bush that evening. In the afternoon, you can see them feeding during their dawn.

A recreated coal mine, as in the 1850s, among the animals at Natureworld.

Coal was mined from near the reserve in the 1850s and lugged by horses on a wooden tramway for loading on ships at Bicheno. The re-created mine with infrastructure including a sail to tunnel air to the miners is an historic drawcard among free-ranging animals.

Bicheno is a splendid holiday and fishing spot with a tough history. European bay whalers after southern right whales and sealers operated from the rocky little harbour here, called The Gulch, from the very early 1800s. Despite their infamous cruelty to the Aborigines, they named the place Waubs Boat Harbour after an Aboriginal "sealers woman" who saved two sealers whose boat overturned 1 km offshore in a storm. In spring, snowdrops bloom by a solitary tombstone in town engraved: *Here lies Waubadebar, female Aborigine of Van Diemens Land. Died June 1832. Aged 40 years. This stone was erected by a few of her White friends.*

The 1832 grave of the heroic Aboriginal woman Waubadebar by Waubs Bay, Bicheno. 'A few of her white friends placed the headstone, but her body was robbed by museum anthropologists.

But, we must reveal, the body of the native heroine does not lie there. In a dark deed in the night in, the curator of a well-known museum dug up Waubadebar's body and stole it for anthropological dissection. The local council's demands for the return of the body evidently were ignored. Waubadebar's memorial is at the coast end of Burgess Street near Waubs Beach at Waubs Bay.

Bicheno immortalises big, fat and jocular James Ebenezer Bicheno, British Colonial Secretary for Van Diemen's Land from 1843 to 1851. The man's trousers were said to be big enough to hold three full bags of flour. He died in office in Hobart, leaving his substantial collection of books to the first Tasmanian library.

Bicheno is a splendid place to stay. Go to the visitor information centre in Burgess Street to find out. North of the town is Diamond Island Nature Reserve, which has one of the coast's scores of colonies of fairy penguins. The nearby Sea Life Centre features the high-and-dry coastal trader *Enterprise*, built in Hobart in 1902, and the anchor from *Otago*, now a rotting skeleton at Otago Bay in Hobart. She was the sole command of Polish-English master novelist Joseph Conrad (1857-1924). One of the few colonial buildings still in town is the simple stone Old Court House and Gaol House, built in 1845. The National Trust classified building has unusual 12-pane windows.

Have a look at the treacherous-looking Gulch, Bicheno's fishing port from where glass-bottom-boat tours operate. The two high walls of stone leading to the wharf are the remains of a giant bin for storing coal shipped from here in the 1850s.

A school group at Bicheno's famous Rocking Rock, 80-tonnes of granite balanced beside the Blowhole, notorious for drenching the intrepid.

The fishing fleet in peril during a storm at The Gulch, Bicheno, in 1972.

Continue south for a few minutes along The Gulch Esplanade to Bicheno's famous blowhole, handily near the Rocking Rock. The huge, 80-tonne hunk of granite is balanced so delicately that it rocks to and fro with the sea in wild weather. The blowhole can go crazy when the surf is up, though, dumping water on sightseers. Only 12 km south from Bicheno on the Tasman Highway is the turn to the left on the C302 for a 27-km trip to **Coles Bay**, which no one visiting

In the pink. A Pacific gull welcomes us to Honeymoon Beach by The Hazards of pink granite at Coles Bay, Freycinet Peninsula.

this island should miss. A few minutes' drive in, Moulting Lagoon is on the right. It usually teems with sea birds, which must have been shedding feathers when the big inlet was named. On the left is the short road to magnificent Friendly Beaches.

South of the Coles Bay resort, majestic peaks of pink granite called The Hazards rear grandly from the usually-blue Tasman Sea in the west and Great Oyster Bay to the east by coastlines punctuated by stretches of fine, white sand. The end of the peninsula is the Freycinet National Park, named after French explorer Baudin's hydrographer. It is one of the prettiest spots on earth; home to pademelons and white-breasted sea eagles. Hundreds of the park's different species of wild flowers include native orchids.

A walk of an hour if you are reasonably fit takes you to the lookout over unforgettable Wineglass Bay. A further hour or so lands you on the beach there. Locals still talk about the day Queen Elizabeth and the Duke of Edinburgh, when cruising up the East Coast in 1988, stopped off at the beach for an Aussie-style barbecue.

Aborigines came to the warmer climate here for millennia and ate shellfish and swans' eggs. They left many middens of shells. The place is named after enterprising loner Silas Cole, who burned a lot of the shells in the mid 1800s to make lime which he sold across the bay at Swansea.

Do take a stroll to magnificent Wineglass Bay, facing the Tasman Sea east of Coles Bay. Courtesy Pure Tasmania, Federal Group.

The kaleidoscope, its colours ever changing, at magnificent Coles Bay.

PART FIVE 120 km
Swansea, Triabunna, Orford
Plus a side trip to Maria Island

Government surveyors Davidson and Mayson and chainman Watson taking a break at Swansea in the 1860s, in the last days of military command, about 40 years after white settlement there. The jetty with its railway was probably still used by bay whalers. Courtesy Spring Bay Glamorgan Historical Society.

YOU MIGHT HAVE the time to visit Friendly Beaches on the way from Coles Bay back to the Tasman Highway. The drive south goes by some fine vineyards and the nation's biggest plantation of walnut trees near **Apslawn** and **Cranbrook** on the 23-km leg to **Swansea.**

A cartload of wattle bark, once used for tanning leather at the old Swansea Bark Mill.

The iconic Morris' General Store in main street Swansea, operating since 1834 and run by the Morris family for more than 100 years.

The first recorded European party around Swansea was on the brig *Mercury*, under Captain John Cox in 1798 on his way from England to Sydney.

He described the timid Aborigines as naked, with dark brown skin and woolly, matted hair. The women carried little bags slung from their shoulders. Caverns had been burned in the bases of trees to make the Aborigines' shelters.

Europeans first settled at Great Oyster Bay in the 1820s and bay whaling gave enterprising settlers like George Meredith a good start. A convict station and military outpost came in 1827. Military command continued at Waterloo Point, around which the village of Swansea grew until the Glamorgan municipality was founded in 1860. Fine examples of dry-stone walls and early stone cottages are all around.

The students would have had to remain immobile for a while in 1905 for this colonial photo at the Swansea State School, built in 1866. Spring Bay Glamorgan Historical Society.

Do visit the former Swansea State School, built in 1866 and the home of the Glamorgan Spring Bay Historical Society on the corner of the main road and Noyes Street. The three-storey Morris' General Store in the main street nearby began life as a one-storey shop in 1834. A plaque in front says Morrises have run the place since 1860. The East

The old school today is the museum of the Glamorgan Spring Bay Historical Society, at the corner of the main street and Noyes Street, next to the RSL club. Photo, Tony Hope.

Coast Museum by the highway north of the town centre has splendid records of the past. It is part of the Swansea Bark Mill (c. 1885) complex where black-wattle bark was processed for tanning leather on an amazing machine that was invented locally.

Stop 7.5 km south of Swansea on the highway to have a look at the intriguing Spiky Bridge. Convicts from the Rocky Hills Probation Station finished building it in 1843 from field stones, laid without mortar. Remains of this station can be seen further south. The spiky stones on top of the parapets were to prevent stock (and probably people) from falling over the sides. Further south are the early estates of Kelvedon and Mayfield with its row of old workmen's cottages and a stone barn by the road.

Beyond interesting old **Little Swanport**, the highway swings inland to rejoin the coast at **Triabunna**, once Temby. Locals claim this was the Aborigines' name for the island's native hen, but there is doubt about that.

Don't miss the amazing Spiky Bridge, 7.5 km south of Swansea. Convicts built it in 1843 with parapets topped by sharp stones, probably to stop animals (and humans?) from falling off.

A former shepherd's slat hut, its shingle roof replaced by corrugated iron, at Little Swanport.

You have probably seen these birds on the Tour. They live around streams and wetlands on most of the island. And only on this island. They are flightless but can swim and run faster than most dogs. About the size of bantams, they have yellow bills, red eyes, green-brown wing feathers with slate grey flanks sporting white flashes.

An Aboriginal lad of Maria Island, early 1800s.

Tasmania's smart and unique native hens are flightless marvels.

Maria Island has a big flock of resident Cape Barren geese.

Their abdomens are usually black. Your authors think these smart critters are under-appreciated treasures. They are too tough to eat, but some oafs shoot them for "sport".

Triabunna's Visitor Information Centre can tell you about the town's visitor facilities and attractions. There is an omnipresent mill, where logs are chipped and piped to ships. This is a destination of trucks laden with logs that you have no doubt encountered.

Little built colonial heritage remains at the town, by sheltered Spring Bay inside Maria Island. John Cox also sailed around here in 1789; then Bass and Flinders circumnavigating the island in 1799 and France's Nicholas Baudin three years later. The military set up a garrison here in 1825 for the new convict station on Maria Island and two of the buildings still stand. It seems the officers did not fancy spending their nights on the lonely isle.

Triabunna grew as a farming and fishing settlement seven years later when Maria Island's prisoners were moved to the new convict colony at Port Arthur. Spring Bay was declared a municipality in 1860. In the early 1900s just north of the town was perhaps the biggest apricot and apple orchard in the southern hemisphere, supplying the Henry Jones cannery in Hobart.

SIDE TRIP

Maria Island

THIS BEAUTIFUL ISLAND steeped in history is another highlight of our Tour. Daily ferries take trippers here from around Triabunna. It is a big island of 260 square kms with hilly north and south sections joined by an isthmus; just like Bruny Island to the south, which is on the Tour later.

Tasmania's Dutch discoverer Abel Tasman evidently had some political ambitions. He named Van Diemen's Land after his boss, the governor of Batavia (now Jakarta), and this island after Van Diemen's wife. Whites plundered its seal population and exploited the Aborigines for many years before and after explorers Cox and Baudin anchored here. The island had one of four whaling stations on the East Coast. The sealers and whalers were known then as Van Demonian sea wolves and wife snatchers. 108,000 seals had been slaughtered around Tasmania by 1803. For years seal skins were Australia's biggest single item of export, mostly to China.

Maria Island, a picturesque new convict station when the island's commissariat clerk T. J. Lempriere painted this water colour of the Commissariat about 1826. Dixson Galleries, State Library of NSW.

Maria, isle of many peaks and on its western shore the Painted Cliffs of stained dolerite. Photo, Tony Hope.

The ubiquitous Governor Lachlan Macquarie picnicked on a little grassy island near Maria in 1821 when he was sailing back to Sydney. He declared it Lachlan's Island "in honour of our dear boy"; his young son Lachlan who was with him, as a parting gesture to Van Diemen's Land before returning to Sydney to mark more locations with his name.

Maria Island's sealers and whalers cleared out when it became a convict station from 1825 to 1832. A second penal probation station operated from 1842 to 1851. Some 800 prisoners then included Irish and New Zealand Maori patriots who opposed conquest by the British Empire. Soldiers recaptured colourful and influential Young Irelander William Smith O'Brien on an eastern beach as he was about to board a longboat to take him to a rescuing Yankee clipper. Many buildings and ruins from the two penal settlements remain. After Port Arthur, this is Tasmania's best built-link with the "convict stain". Both places are in line for World Heritage listing.

Ruins from cement works operated by flamboyant Angelo Guillio Diego Bernacchi in the late 1880s and a later short-lived cement works in the 1920s are near the jetty. The Italian silk merchant leased the whole island for a shilling (10c) a year and planted 50,000 grape vines. He established a silkworm farm, orchards, a hotel and a coffee palace. Although he had the large jail, or separate apartments building, demolished and used the materials for other buildings, we tourers owe Bernacchi a debt for the preservation of the other buildings which he used to house his employees. The horror with which Tasmanians of previous generations regarded their convict family connections was illustrated when Bernacchi addressed a dinner party of Hobart dignitaries. The Italian flourished a leather-bound journal listing details of the Maria Island's former convicts. "Shall we see what your ancestors came here for?" he asked his startled audience.

The journal was the sole item stolen when Bernacchi's home was broken into soon after. In 1953, the book of fear was quietly and anonymously given to a records office in England by, we assume, a descendant of the robber.

Maria Island is a National Park, well maintained by the Parks and Wildlife Service, which also has a visitor information centre there. It has resident flocks of fairly-tame Cape Barren geese. An offshore area is a flourishing marine reserve. Geological features include marine fossils and colourful iron-stained sandstone. Looking from the sheltered western shore, the spectacular Painted Cliffs show layers of sediment and ancient dolerite which formed the island's four mountains. On the eastern side, they sheer from a great height into the sea.

✳✳✳

THE SEASIDE RESORT of **Orford** is only 9 km down the Tasman Highway from Triabunna. It was named after England's Earl of Orford. Refreshingly, the Prosser River and Prosser Bay were named after Thomas Prosser; a convict on the run, we're told.

There is an interesting walk of about 30 minutes from near the northern side of the bridge over the Prosser along the Old Convict Road, where convicts sweated in the mid 1800s.

A foot track between Shelly and Spring Beaches south of the river goes to a large sandstone quarry overgrown with trees. Stone hewn from here over 20 years from 1870 was shipped in blocks to help construct many buildings, including the Melbourne Law Courts and Post Office.

PART SIX 90 km
Little Gondwana, Dunalley, Eaglehawk Neck, Port Arthur

Cliffs of sandstone plunging to the sea are common on the lower East Coast.

A MARVELLOUS TRIP is ahead on a gravel road in good condition (at least as we write this) through native forests and farmland overlooking the coast with a stop at what we call Little Gondwana.

Cross the bridge over the Prosser River at Orford, continue 1 km ahead along Rheban Road and turn right onto Wielangta Forest Road. 15 km gets you to the Wielangta State Forest reserve and the old Robertson Bridge. This is an historic icon in itself, made from about 1,200 metres of blue gum logs. It crosses little Sandspit River.

Do stop at the parking area about 100 metres on the left past the bridge. Across the road a boardwalk takes you on an easy 15-minute stroll into the captivating valley Little Gondwana. It is like stepping into pre-history, surrounded by giant myrtle, sassafras and blackwood trees, lichens, tree ferns 10 metres tall and, by the river, sandstone caves which surely were retreats for Aborigines. This sheltered spot seems to have survived unchanged from when Tasmania was part of the super-continent Gondwana.

Parts of the land, once tropical, periodically broke away from Antarctica 130 billion years ago. They drifted north to form today's South America, Africa, India and, finally, Australia. We're still heading north, actually; at the speed your finger nails grow, about 3 cm a year.

The walkway passing here under a ledge of rock in a place of pre-history, amazing "Little Gondwana", south of Orford by the Wielangta Forest Road.

The timber-milling settlement of Wielangta, with wooden tramlines, a bakery, general store, a school, a dance hall and a bush pub, thrived around here for 20 years from about 1915.

Dunalley's memorial to Dutch explorer of 1642 Abel Tasman, who evidently never came ashore at the place he named Van Diemen's Land.

Turn left on to Bream Creek Road to go through magnificent farmland with coastal views to **Bream Creek**. 17 km from Little Gondwana, turn left on the sealed road down the slope for 3 km to lovely **Marion Bay** beside Blackman Bay. Beware, as the sign here warns, of wandering wombats. You join the A9 Arthur Highway on the outskirts of **Dunalley**. Imlay Street on the left near the school takes you to the Abel Tasman Monument, recording the explorer's carpenter's planting of his nation's flag across the bay on 3 December 1642 and claiming this land for the Netherlands. A

The historic canal at Dunalley, looking towards the bridge to the Tasman Peninsula.

A bronze eagle by the canal.

claim which, of course, the English ignored. But the land Tasman claimed was a small island he thought was part of the mainland.

The lively history of Dunalley is presented in a shelter in the park in the town by the Denison Canal. This was gouged over three years from 1902 as a safer and shorter route for boats going between the East Coast and Norfolk Bay rather than going around the Tasman Peninsula. A pioneer Irish farmer named the town after Baron Dunalley in 1838. The Dunalley Hotel, on the right across the bridge on the way to Port Arthur, was built in 1866.

You have joined the Convict Trail through the Forestier Peninsula to Port Arthur. The peninsula's sole town is little old **Murdunna** by Norfolk Bay, a former relief station for colonial travellers. Its name is Aboriginal for a star, selected at random from a list of sweet-sounding indigenous monikers used to dub places when Governor Macquarie was not around.

Turn left at the top of a rise on to Pirates Bay Drive for a marvellous view of the Tasman Sea, Pirates Bay and Eaglehawk Neck. The drive wends from the lookout down through rain forest to the art deco Lufra Country Hotel. Inns had been on this site since the late 1800s. When aviation and Pioneer bus tour operator Sir Reginald Ansett arrived in 1948 he declared the outlook from here "the best view the world" and built today's grand premises. The shoreline permian-age rocks across the road have weathered into a freak pattern you should see. The oddity is called the Tesselated Pavement.

From the lookout over Pirates Bay. Eaglehawk Neck is on the right.

The isthmus a little south is the once notorious **Eaglehawk Neck**, which connects mainland Tasmania with the rugged and infamous Tasman Peninsula, teeming with tales of the colonial convict days. Some of that history is shown off at the Neck's Officers' Quarters Museum.

A bronze mastiff on its site today is a graphic reminder of the ferocious dog line, which most escaping convicts had to face. Sculpted 1999 by Ruth Waterhouse & Curtis Hore.

Governor Arthur chose the peninsula for his main penal settlement because it was an isolated virtual island with handy access by sea from Hobart Town. Convicts were told the waters around here were thick with sharks, ready to eat escapers who tried to swim to freedom. So their only land passage to liberty was by Eaglehawk Neck. To discourage this, a row of kennels was installed from the seashore, across the isthmus and extending on anchored floats well into Eaglehawk Bay to the west. At every kennel was a fierce dog. They were on chains just short enough to prevent the hounds fighting one another. Day and night nearby were soldiers with muskets. However, convict Martin Cash and his accomplices Lawrence Cavenagh and George Jones swam across Eaglehawk Bay on the night of Boxing Day 1842. It was Cash's second escape from Port Arthur. We present tales of the trio's rampaging later.

Governor Sir John Franklin (nephew of Matthew Flinders) and Lady Jane inspecting the dog line at Eaglehawk Neck about 1840.

One of the very few escapees, however, had inside knowledge. An enterprising convict named William Cripps was sentenced to the lash for selling on the black market flour he stole from ingredients he cooked. So he took off from Port Arthur, evaded his hunters and, one night, arrived at the Neck's dreaded dog line.

Cripps walked up to the canine cordon to be greeted by an array of wagging tails. The dogs knew and liked him. For William was a former Eaglehawk dog handler. He let two dogs loose. They followed him past the soldiers' shed and into the forest to the north.

The dogs helped him do quite nicely on the loose for 18 months catching and trapping forester kangaroos and wallabies. He built a hut of bark. Now and then Cripps sneaked back past the friendly dog line to Port Arthur to steal food including more flour for baking bread. He was caught by chance by a soldier who also happened to be the stolen dogs' owner. The Imperial Government auctioned 1,800 bundled kangaroo and wallaby skins found at Cripps' hut while the errant cook copped 100 lashes. We think he later went to

Norfolk Island but William Cripps saw out his days a free man in Hobart Town. Your authors can't prove a connection, but we can note with their blessing that a prominent and multi-generational family of bakers in Hobart today is called Cripps.

SNAPSHOT c. 1840
"I'm not a kangaroo!"

OUR RECORDS of this event are flimsy, but your authors understand that Billy Hunt was a "strolling actor", a sort of wandering minstrel, in England in the early 1800s when he was transported to Van Diemen's Land for petty theft. Here is our version of his moment of fame:

Pining for the open road, Billy escaped from a work gang at Port Arthur. The surf on the beach roared in his ears as he crouched in the trees overlooking the Eaglehawk dog line, wondering how to get away from this peninsula of pain in paradise. Billy decided to use his acting skills.

Somehow the entertainer killed, or found dead, a forester kangaroo. He skinned it, leaving the tail attached. He wrapped the animal's skin over his convict clothes and crowned himself with the head. He figured that the dogs, trained to harass escapers, were not likely to get excited about another loping kangaroo after they had been fed. The sun had set over Eaglehawk Bay when Billy the kangaroo quietly hopped along the beach and past the slumbering dogs. The freedom of the scrub lay before him.

Meanwhile, a soldier sat on a log near his cabin nursing a musket and contemplating the gathering night. Suddenly, he spotted movement on the beach. It was a big boomer kangaroo, only 40 metres distant. Here was good, fresh tucker. The soldier fired at his quarry. The blast woke some 20 dogs. They bolted from their kennels to the limit of their chains, barking and growling with a terrifying blood lust.

The soldier's blast had missed. His finger was on the trigger for a second shot. He froze, bewildered, as the boomer raised both its paws and pulled off its head! "I'm not a *kangaroo*!" it cried. "Don't shoot. It's only me, Billy Hunt."

Other soldiers rushed out of the cabin and fell about laughing. Billy the actor was returned to Port Arthur and flogged. But he had won comic celebrity status with his fellow convicts.

***

WE RECOMMEND that you take the first turn to the left south from the Neck for a drive through a remarkable collection of holiday shacks called **Doo Town** and then to some gobsmacking features of the sea cliffs. Follow the signs on the C338 Blowhole Road beside Pirates Bay to see the wonders of the Tasman Blowhole, Tasman Arch and the often-roiling Devils Kitchen beside Waterfall Bay. This area through to Port Arthur has a multitude of fine places to stay and dine.

Back on the A9, 9 km south beside pretty Norfolk Bay, is the old settlement of **Taranna**. The main building here was a commissariat store, then a hotel. It is now the Norfolk Bay Convict Station b.& b.

Australia's very first railway ran from here from 1837. It carried non-convict passengers, stores and even coal for about 7 km to and from the Port Arthur penal station on wooden tracks. Most of the arriving cargo came on ships from Hobart Town which tied up in the sheltered bay at Taranna. And why use valuable horses or oxen to propel the wooden railway's box cars when there was such a supply of convicts? After all, the wretches had become used to being shackled like beasts of burden to plough furrows on new fields on the peninsula. Four running convicts pushed each box car. At least they could jump on board to ride down hills. Also at Taranna, you can get up close to wildlife and local flora at the Tasmanian Devil Conservation Park.

Nearby on the left is the superb Federation Chocolate factory and Museum, in a building cut by convicts and operated by the Tatnell family since the early 1900's. The museum reveals more about local timber industry history.

Road signs will direct you to the car park at the **Port Arthur** Historic Site. The first and last place to visit at this most extensive reminder of Australia's convict years should be the site's comprehensive gift shop, near the restaurant and Visitor Information Centre. Port Arthur and the Tasmanian Museum and Art Gallery in Hobart are the most visited attractions in the State, proving the supreme general interest in our history.

The penal station was established in 1830 as a place for convicts to cut and mill timber. A few years later it became a punishment centre for repeat offenders from all parts of the island and Sydney. There were more than 2,000 convicts, civil staff and soldiers here by 1840. Most of the prisoners were employed constructing buildings and the colony's ships, making bricks and shoes and clothing and even brooms. Vegetable and flower gardens abounded. Excellent guided tours of the site and its buildings are available. After it was closed all salvageable parts of the settlement were sold off and sparks from bushfires on the dry shingle roofs destroyed most of the rest. Few bothered to protect it. At the time it was considered a good thing for this infamous re-

This striking silhouette of a tree feller is outside the Federation Chocolate Factory and timber museum at Taranna.

minder of the past to be reduced to ashes. What you see are a few of the surviving and restored buildings and ruins.

Only a small percentage of convicts were sent to Port Arthur. Most of them fared reasonably well and later became free citizens, the ancestors of a goodly slice of Tasmania's population today. But many episodes of rank horror and abominations still echo among the ruins and colonial buildings many people swear are haunted by restless spirits.

Dignitaries seldom had to walk from Taranna to old Port Arthur. Litho. by W.L. Walton after Lt. Colonel Godfrey Mundy, 1852.

Perhaps the saddest scenes were across Carnarvon Bay at the Point Puer prison where at times 800 boys transported across the world, some as young as six, were incarcerated in shanty sheds. They received basic schooling and trades training under severe discipline.

A notable victim of England's pitiless law courts sent to Point Puer was Tom Rares. This child of the London slums was transported in 1832 to seven years of incarceration for stealing one apple. He was aged nine. After serving his seven years, Tom was told he faced another seven at Point Puer for alleged misdemeanors. He escaped the next day, sneaked by the dog line and eventually crossed the Derwent in a rowboat he stole. He lived for a while foraging and hiding in a shed behind Hobart Town's Man of Ross Hotel. With the police in pursuit Tom, now aged 16, fled north and became a bushranger. When raiding a farm with others near Launceston, now-brazen Tom shot off his own right hand when his gun exploded.

He was caught and promptly tried in Launceston while nearly dead, we're told, from loss of blood. Next day, still semi-conscious, young Tom Rares was hanged. All for an apple.

The first batch of 68 boys to go to Point Puer evidently at least had a merry time on the way. They staggered from the ship from Hobart rotten drunk from drinking six dozen bottles of wine, destined we understand for Port Arthur's administrators. You can drive to Point Puer on the C347 Safety Cove Road but only rubble from the mainly-timber boys' prison settlement remains. The road also goes to aptly-named Remarkable Cave, shaped like a map of Tasmania, from where you can see impressive Cape Raoul.

The station entered an era of welfare when convict transportation ended in 1853 after Van Diemen's Land had received 67,000 prisoners. Some 14,000 were women. After 1853 the former prison housed the debris of the system, some mental and physical wrecks not able to look after themselves. The settlement closed in 1877 after housing about 12,000 prisoners and their guards.

A sketch of Port Arthur in its early prime in 1845. By Lieut. Charles Hext. From Old Tasmanian Prints, *Clifford Craig.*

The penal station in 1872, before fire wiped out most of it, including the roof of the church. Photo, John Beattie. Black & White Photographics.

The Port Arthur Penitentiary today.

Ruins you can explore

Governor Arthur

The Port Arthur site has a garden in memory of probably the nation's worst massacre here in April 1996 when mentally-warped gunman Martin Bryant killed 35 people and wounded more.

Do, however, take a cruise to the nearby Isle of the Dead! About 1,100 people were buried on this 2.5 hectare spot in the bay during convict times. Even in death, the high ground was for civil and military personnel, with tombstones. Dumped with quicklime in unmarked trenches in the low ground near the jetty were the bodies of convicts and local paupers and lunatics. Resident gravedigger convict John Barrow grew well-fertilised flowers. But only flowers. He could not eat vegetables from that soil, the lonely Barrow declared.

In 1837 a commissariat clerk carved the shape of a horizontal arrow into the face of a small cliff at the north of the Isle of the Dead to record the high-tide level. This marker is valued today by scientists checking tidal fluctuations caused by global warming.

In an act of regretted bravado, Michael Tatlow sailed to this island reputedly teeming with ghosts and walked alone through the scrub at 11.45 on the night of December 31, 1997, for a New Year with the spooks. Clouds scudded before a breeze in the moonlight, casting a concert of moving shadows as he sat on a tombstone. Things rattled and squeaked and sometimes crashed in the bushes. Possums? he hoped fearfully. "I got my spooky New Year," Michael recalls. "I walked back down the wooded track at a fast rate, not looking back, feeling strongly that I was not alone, hairs at the back of my neck actually prickling. A cry I heard was surely from a bird. I smartly cast off and found my cat of black, usually a gregarious critter, cowering and scared under a bunk. Never again." You go there in daylight and not alone.

Tombstones of the upper classes on the high ground of the Isle of the Dead, a spooky place at night, as Mike Tatlow attests.

PART SEVEN 130 km
Nubeena, Premaydena, Sorell, Richmond, Hobart

Teams of convicts had the task of bullocks or horses to plough new ground on the Tasman Peninsula. This painting, recreated from the Beattie collection, may have a fanciful addition of the ball attached to the whip wielded by the overseer goading his herd.

DRIVING A LOOP around the Tasman Peninsula before heading for Hobart is rewarding, as Port Arthur is only part of the peninsula's convict experience. The distances are short and packed with history.

Take the B37 Nubeena Road for 11 kms west to **Nubeena**, Aboriginal for crayfish, often called rock lobster nowadays. This pretty seaside resort, the largest town on the peninsula, was a convict timber-getting centre in the 1830s and steadily grew through farming and fishing.

17 km north is the former convict probation station of Impression Bay, now **Premaydena**, which has some remaining colonial buildings of a once-large settlement of 600 convicts and staff in the 1840s. Turn left here on the C341 for a drive of about 10 kms to Saltwater River to see the remains of another large probation station.

Further west are the beautiful sandstone ruins of the infamous Coal Mines buildings. This was the dreaded place of punishment for about eight years from 1835 for the peninsula's "refractory" convicts. You can wander among the ruins and look at the small and gloomy underground prison cells. Take the road around the back and see the remains of the main shaft to the mine and further west an air vent. Convicts with only picks in flickering candle-light had to lay flat to hack at coal in seams less than a metre deep. With Port Arthur, the site is in line for World Heritage listing.

A horror job, even for convicts, was in the shallow seams of the island's first, filthy coal mines at Saltwater River.

Complete our loop of the peninsula through the former Cascades probation station for convicts at **Koonya**, with its interesting museum and restored colonial buildings. Turn left onto the Arthur Highway towards Eaglehawk Neck at Taranna. Some 10 km past Dunalley, stop at the fascinating Colonial Convict Collection folk and history museum at the village of **Copping**. It also has a visitor

Wanted! This 1843 poster in the Colonial Convict Collection folk and history museum at Copping promises a fortune then, and a Conditional Pardon for any convict, for a lead to capturing bushranging escapees from Port Arthur, Martin Cash and his mates Jones and Cavanagh.

information service. Some of the oddball folk exhibits here gathered over the years are fascinating and the working models will give you a laugh.

The highway continues west to **Sorell**, another of Tasmania's significant towns with strong bonds with the past. Governor Macquarie visited here in 1821 with Southern V.D.L. Governor Sorell. In typical fashion, Macquarie smartly changed the spot's name from Pittwater to Sorell. It was an important grain-growing centre from 1815 to the 1860s. Rampaging bushranger Matthew Brady and his gang took over Sorell in 1824. They released prisoners from the lockup, replacing them with the guards and rode off laden with grog. The town has many gracious old buildings you should see.

Taking the road past the airport to Hobart requires a left turn at the traffic lights in Sorell, but importantly our Tour continues directly ahead on the A3 towards old **Buckland**. A few kms from Sorell, though, go left on the bitumen C351 Brinktop Road through farms and scenic bushland to a jewel in

The 1841 Scots (now Uniting) Church in Sorell has a chimney flue disguised as a turret beside the tower.

Richmond's famous old bridge over the Coal River, the historic Catholic Church among the trees. Photo, David Wooley.

Tasmania's basket of old treats, **Richmond**. It was earlier known as Sweet Water Hills. Until the causeways were built across Pittwater in 1872, Richmond was on the main route between Hobart and the East Coast and Tasman Peninsula.

The 1823 stone bridge you cross to enter the main town is Australia's oldest bridge still in use. Stop here and enjoy a stroll by the Coal River, named because a little coal was found in the valley upstream in 1803, only weeks after Europeans first settled in Van Diemen's Land. The beautiful spired St Johns Church, embowered by trees near the river to the north, was completed in 1836. It is generally called the nation's oldest Catholic church. But we have visited St Brigids Catholic Church at Millers Point, Sydney, which opened a year earlier than St Johns. St Brigids was closed at times between 1874-80, however. So St Johns is Australia's oldest *continuously-used* place of Catholic worship. St Johns is usually open for inspection. Its designer was former convict Frederick Thomas. The church and the bridge glow from floodlights at night.

The courtyard at Old Richmond Gaol, the nation's oldest intact prison. The men's solitary cells are behind the tree.

The whole town turned out in 1924 to celebrate their bridge's 100th birthday.

Reliving the day the Richmond bridge opened.

Exploring the streets of Richmond is fascinating. They have a marvellous collection of mostly Georgian stone and timber homes, shops and public buildings making it what your authors rate the most and the best Georgian village in the nation. 45 buildings are registered on the National Estate. A mill, now Mill House private residence just east of the bridge, was built in 1815 to make flour from local wheat crops which supplied New South Wales as well. Have a look inside The Granary, a relic of this period built with the same technology as used in rural buildings 1,000 years ago. The 1835 court house in the main street and the primary school (c. 1834) are also claimed to be the oldest in Australia.

For a graphic insight into convict history do not miss the fascinating Old Richmond Gaol in Bathurst Street. Built in 1825, it pre-dates Port Arthur by five years and is the oldest standing prison in the nation. Local crooks were kept here, often manacled to eight-kilo. balls of iron. It was designed for 60 prisoners but often held 100. Men were in the west wing and women in the east wing of a courtyarded complex, the work of architect John Lee Archer. There is also a flogging block. As your authors have done, you can close yourself in the utter blackness of solitary confinement cells. Men and women were kept in the cells for up to a month fed on only bread and water. The records and relics of the institution's inglorious past include the tale of inmate Ikey Soloman, upon whom Charles Dickens based the *Oliver Twist* character Fagin, the "fence" for urchin child thieves in London.

Playing giants ... your authors survey the marvellous model of their home patch as it was in the 1820s at Richmond's Old Hobart Town Model Village. Photo, David Wooley.

To get a superb taste of colonial Hobart, walk around a meticulous model of how it looked in the 1820s at the Old Hobart Town Model Village, off the main street. Also see the National Trust's Oak Lodge with its wonderful 19th century cottage garden. Richmond has several fine art and souvenir outlets such as the old Saddlers Court Gallery. An innovative resort, loved especially by children, is ZooDoo Wildlife Park, 7 kms north-west on the C322 from the western edge of the town. The animals you can "safari" to include white wallabies, breeding Tasmanian devils, buffaloes, camels, koalas, cheeky emus and, a new headliner, a couple of Bengal tigers.

The heart of the Coal Valley Wine Region, with several cellars for tastings of outstanding vintages including the Meadowbank Estate's gallery and restaurant in the vine groves, is beside the B31 Richmond Road south of Richmond on the way to Hobart.

At **Cambridge**, the airport is 12 km away to the left. But we take the right turn to go through the old hamlet with its pub, and a former early inn a little farther along the road. The B31 connects through an underpass to the Tasman Highway.

Among the European trees on the slope before you on the Tasman Bridge over the River Derwent at **Hobart** is towered Government House, the home of the island's 27th governor, Tasmania's representative of the Queen. The grand neo-gothic mansion of sandstone, with 70 rooms and completed in 1859, is said to be her favorite antipodean residence. It is one of the finest vice-regal houses in the former British Empire. Not bad for Australia's smallest state. Unlike colonial days of Imperial appointments, the State Government recommends governors, now former Chief Justice Peter Underwood.

The Harbour, Hobart Town in 1830, eight years after convicts built the causeway to Hunter Island, home to the buildings near the ships and a place of public hangings. Litho by St. Aulaire after de Sainson.

Astride the mighty Derwent, more a harbour here than a river, and ringed by wooded hills and Mt Wellington, Hobart (pop. just over 200,000) is the second oldest after Sydney and surely the loveliest capital city in the nation. It also has a wondrous number of colonial buildings looking much as they did 150 years or so ago.

The best way to plan your stay in Hobart is to consult the Tasmanian Travel and Information Centre near the waterfront on the corner of Davey and Elizabeth Streets.

You can also get at the centre, and at other outlets in the city, the top-selling book *A Walk in Old Hobart* by two of your authors, Charles and Michael. Peter Mercer was their vital guide in the tricky business of candidly writing history. *A Walk in Old Hobart* takes you, with a fold-out map, on a walk of two hours or so around the historic waterfront, the unique colonial suburb of Battery Point and the city. It shows off with photographs old and new Hobart's buildings with sometimes-irreverent tales about characters and events that made it the gem it is today.

Quite a transition, it is, from its first couple of decades after white settlement, when it was known as The Camp. The town's name honours Lord Hobart, England's Secretary of State for War and the Colonies at the time of settlement. Again, the boss of the namer.

Seals of bronze, part of an enchanting display about Antarctic exploration, greet the dawn and three old ladies of sail at the Hobart wharves, Enterprise, Rhona H *and* Endeavour Replica.

Naval officer John Bowen, aged 23, settled at Risdon Cove on the river's eastern shore in September 1803 with a rag-tag party of convicts and soldiers. Many of them were the scum of Sydney's troublesome soldiers and prisoners; men the first city was glad to be rid of.

Army officer David Collins led a second, bigger and smarter party which settled across the river where Hobart is today in February 1804. They came from England after a brief stay at Port Phillip (today's Melbourne), which Collins decided was unfit for human

Your authors at Kellys Steps, Salamanca Place.

habitation. The party of nearly 300 convicts, some 100 guards, about 30 free settlers and several wives and children, was hand-picked for their skills. They included farmers, five fishers, 12 cobblers, nine sawyers and some carpenters. There were a couple of Dutchmen, a German, a Pole, a Portugese, a French confectioner, an Afro-American violinist, 17 Irish men and women, about 10 Scots and Welsh, and five London Jews. So, with such roots, multiculturalism is not all that new. The convicts were aged from nine, yes nine, to 57.

It seems to your authors that, although fortuitous for Van Demon's Land, Collins' arrival was a high-handed incursion on young Bowen's patch, which the newcomers smartly usurped. London's Colonial Office had expected Collins to settle by Bass Strait and he went to Port Phillip to give the English a footing in the south of the continent partly in case the French staked a claim there. Collins took it upon himself to sail on to the Derwent, carrying a letter from Governor-in-chief King ordering his man Bowen to yield command to the army officer.

Few people seem to know that Bowen had called his settlement Hobart, not Risdon Cove, on King's instructions. Collins, with some authority we understand, pinched the name by calling *his* settlement Hobart Town. Van Diemen's Land had four settlements of whites, two in the south and two in the north, by late 1804 compared with only one on mainland Australia.

Collins and co. sailed up the Derwent marvelling at thousands of black swans and mobs of wallabies, kangaroos and emus. The pioneers' hunting dogs found the little Tasmanian emus to be easy meat. They were early contributors to the birds' speedy extinction. But at least Collins forbade the killing of tasty swans in December 1804, just when his charges were planning their Christmas dinners. Hunting dogs were so valued in the colony that a good hound would fetch a price for which a labourer would work for years.

The Quay, Hobart Town, c. 1875. This scene by J.J. Crewe shows colonial wharfies loading barrels of whale oil at what is now Salamanca Place. Tasmaniana Library, State Library of Tasmania.

Collins described Bowen's convicts as "abandoned, hardened wretches". His army-led settlers west of the river related pretty well with the Aborigines but remained aloof from the eastern shore's navy-led strugglers, blamed for the "Risdon massacre" near the settlement of May 1804 while John Bowen was away. The truth of it is still debated, but we understand that two or three, perhaps friendly, perhaps threatening, natives were shot.

Rather than annoy Aboriginal activists on land returned to their community at Risdon Cove, even the State Government has ignored the fact of Bowen's landing. Major celebrations were held to mark the 200th anniversary of the first settlement of whites. They were in February 2004, amazingly recognising only Collins' pioneers. Poor Bowen's lot, who came five months earlier, were never officially mentioned.

The Chain Gang of convicts, Hobart Town, c. 1830. Etching after Edward Backhouse from James Backhouse's Narrative.

Hangings were common in old Hobart Town. The sight of bodies swinging from the gallows on Hunter Island, now part of Hobart's waterfront, was pretty common for the first few years. And also a warning to arriving convicts, sailors and settlers that this was a penal town with swift "justice" for crooks. Welcome to Hobart Town.

The majority of hangings were for theft, not murder. In a spree of killings in 1826-27, Governor Arthur, the founder of Port Arthur, had 103 men and women hanged. 260 were executed during his term, chilling the population into submission. The long-bar gallows at the first big prison in the town could drop a job lot of 13 victims. It was at the south-west corner diagonally opposite today's St David's Anglican Cathedral, where Murray and Macquarie Streets meet, the sole remaining city intersection of Georgian buildings in the nation.

Gentry from England who were granted free land along with convict labourers and servants introduced the notion of exclusively-owned private property in Van Diemen's Land.

Old Wharf, Hobarton, in 1856, drawn from in front of the Customs House (now Parliament House). To the left, the Customs House Hotel at the end of Murray Street. The hotel corner is just the same today. From Butler Stoney's A residence in Tasmania.

A rare portrait of three of the last full-blood Tasmanian Aborigines. From the left, Truganini (aged 65), William Lanne (26) and Pinnanobathac (about 50) in 1866. Photographed in Hobart by Charles A. Woolley. Courtesy of Lewis Woolley.

They did not want Aborigines roaming on their estates. This led to conflict and bloodshed. So, at the property owners' urging, Governor Arthur in 1830 delivered the infamous Black Line of soldiers, convicts and volunteers to line up across much the island to drive out the first Tasmanians. The project caught only an old man and a boy.

Hundreds of southern right whales frolicked and calved in the Derwent estuary in winter months until shore-based whalers harpooned the last of them in 1852. Once, rowing a boat on the Derwent risked being capsized by a cavorting denizen. Whales have inherited memories, it seems. They seldom visit the river.

Convict transportation to Van Diemen's Land ended in 1853. A few years later, the colony was renamed Tasmania, hopefully to erase its "convict stain". The settlement's "kangaroo economy" ended in the 1830s. Hobart became a booming town growing rich from selling seal skins, whale oil, provisioning ships, agriculture and, later, manufacturing.

Do take a walk, not a drive, along Salamanca Place and then around marvellous Battery Point, where your authors Michael and

Hobart's Wrest Point tower by the Derwent. Courtesy, Federal Group.

Charles live (and Mike was born). It is a village within a city, by far Australia's outstanding centre of intact 19th century, mostly Georgian buildings and rich with ripper yarns of the past. Its name comes from a colonial gun battery near the shore at Princes Park, installed to repel feared sea invaders from France, Russia and even America, with which England, thus this colony, was at war. Fortunately, the gun battery never had to fire a shot in anger. It was farcically useless.

A big mast at today's park was Hobart's end of a complex of semaphore signal stations that sent shipping and other news to and from Port Arthur. Word of an escaping convict or that the soldiers' pay was on the way from Hobart was transmitted in a few minutes. A replica semaphore mast and a plaque of information about the system is at the park.

Magnificent red brick and sandstone Gattonside on Sandy Bay Road, Battery Point. The mansion, built by Henry Hunter c. 1885, is now a luxury b. & b.

For a taste of life in an elegant residence of the 1830s, visit Battery Point's Narryna Heritage Museum in Hampden Road. Peter Mercer is a member of the committee of volunteers who manage Narryna and has written a hand-book about it. And for a taste of good amber brew by walls decorated with photographs of old Hobart and its maritime history, call at the 1846 Shipwrights Arms Hotel in Colville Street. Battery Point resident Andrew Inglis Clark (1848-1907) was a barrister, politician and judge who was the prime architect of Australia's Constitution and co-devised the State's democratic Hare-Clark electoral system, now adopted in many parts of the world.

⇥ THE FLASH MOB ⇤

Some 300 women convicts at the Female Factory, now a fascinating attraction at South Hobart, in 1844 reportedly revolted against their hypocritical chaplain by baring their naked bottoms in front of a bewildered Governor Franklin and his amused wife, Lady Jane. Artist, Peter Gouldthorpe.

The Tasmanian Museum and Art Gallery, in Macquarie Street near the old sandstone Town Hall and the GPO, is the State's most-visited attraction. The museum, where Peter Mercer was Curator of History for 23 years, has a diverse exhibition of early memorabilia and paintings.

Do visit the remains of the Female Factory in South Hobart, where women convicts were incarcerated from 1828. It was one of four in the colony and is the best preserved. The last prisoners left

Tyre kickers. Used car sales at Kennedys, Salamanca Place, c. 1912.
Colin Dennison Collection.

there in 1877, when it became a Home for Imperial Lunatics! That sounds like mad monarchs. But the patients were mentally impaired people whose care was the responsibility of the Crown. The Factory closed in 1904. It is one of 11 sites in Australia (five of them in Tasmania) nominated for World Heritage listing.

Other centres you should see include the pioneers' tombstones with graphic inscriptions in St David's Park, the long-established Royal Tasmanian Botanical Gardens, the Penitentiary Chapel Historic Site in Campbell Street, the Maritime Museum of Tasmania near Constitution Dock at the corner of Argyle and Davey Streets, the Anglesea Barracks and Military Museum in upper Davey Street, and the Allport and Crowther collections of Tasmanian books, art and photographs at the Tasmanian Public Library in Murray Street.

New Town is studded with grand old houses on what were once small country estates and now overwhelmed by suburbia. One of them you should see is the National Trust's Georgian villa Runnymede. In upper Lenah Valley is a small replica of an ancient Greek temple built for Lady Franklin as a museum in the early 1840s. The beautiful old orphanage buildings each side of St Johns Church, New Town, are among Hobart's gems.

The top of Mt Wellington is only 20 minutes' drive from the CBD for your first feel of alpine Tasmania, perhaps some snow, and in clear weather captivating views of the city, the Derwent estuary and south-eastern Tasmania's mountainous topography. Explorer George Bass scaled the trackless mountain in 1798 and gave a still-feathered swan he had shot on the Derwent to an Aborigine he met. Your authors wonder what the dickens Bass was doing lugging a big black swan on that gruelling climb.

And yes, Governor Macquarie struck here in a big way. He bestowed his own name on the then-main street. Elizabeth and Campbell Streets immortalised his wife, the former Elizabeth Campbell. Visitors who were enchanted by old Hobart Town and wrote rapturously about it include Mark Twain, Anthony Trollope and Charles Darwin. The city's most famous son, we reckon, was swashbuckling Errol Flynn (1909-59), who starred in more than 50 films, mostly out of Hollywood.

Hobart was a busy port in the late 1800s. New Wharf, Hobarton.
Black & White Photographics.

SNAPSHOT 1815

A hell in paradise

IN THIS CAPTURE of a day in Hobart's past, imagine you are at the intersection of Elizabeth and Macquarie Streets, by today's GPO, the Town Hall and Franklin Square, one sunny afternoon on Christmas Eve 1815.

You arrived from London for a new life in this land of opportunity as a free settler three years ago after months of seasickness and fear on the barque *Indefatigable*, the first ship to bring convicts to the colony directly from England.

You will never forget the frightening horror as your ship sidled up near little Hunter Island at the sight of the bodies of two men strung up on gallows there. Convicts, whom the redcoat soldiers trooped ashore from their stinking quarters, quaked at the sight.

Children are at play here, dodging around horse dung and horse-drawn gigs and carts and the sawn-off stump of a mighty eucalypt left in the middle of the road. Governor Davey's men nail public notices on it. And foolhardy commoners sometimes plant notes of complaint there, too. One silly fellow was caught doing that lately. He was tied screaming to the stump and flayed with 100 lashes. Corruption in government has spawned on the island; likely to fester for generations, you fear.

A new notice is nailed on the stump. It declares martial law in the colony, giving the governor unlimited power and promising execution to bushrangers, escaped convicts who are marauding about, stealing from farmhouses. It reminds you that eight years ago the head of the murderous bushranger Richard Lemon was paraded around here on a stick as a warning and as proof to the public that Lemon's roving days were over.

You buy a copy of the new *Van Diemen's Land Gazette* from a ticket-of-leave woman selling them by the stump. You read of the horse races at the new track New Town, that a once-a-week mail service by lone horsemen will operate soon between Hobart and

Launceston, and that a young mariner called James Kelly set out 12 days ago with four oarsmen on little *Elizabeth* for a voyage of exploration right around the island.

This is a merry day for the free settlers, the minority in the colony. The children anticipate gifts tonight. "Father Christmas might bring me a new doll!", an excited girl tells her friends. "And I might get a pair of *boots!*" a boy in bare feet responds. "We're having a whole leg of emu tomorrow for dinner", another counters. Two ladies in the simple, flowing Regency style of the day and bonnets ride by in a gig full of Christmas shopping.

Tonight you will join your fellow coopers who make barrels for ale and the oil from whales that romp in the river in winter. It will be big night of brown rum and ale at the Whale Fishery (later the Hope & Anchor Tavern).

You have adjusted to this land of opposites at the ends of the earth, where December is warm and July is cold. Where the animals and trees are so strange. Where the tigers look more like dogs. Where the swans are black, not white as they are on the Thames. You no longer fear those black devils that scream in the bush at night, their eyes glowing red in the light of your lantern. The cries of the gulls, different from those in the Old Country, no longer sound alien. You smile at the memory of Christmases in the snow in dreary and slummy old London Town.

This is a challenging and enchanting land, teeming with the opportunities you sought. The soil is fertile, there is timber galore and surely this island is rich in minerals. Your future looks bright in this sort of raw hell of a town in paradise.

***

The Eastern Shore

WHILE IN HOBART, we suggest you return to the Eastern Shore, an often-overlooked part of Tasmania's heritage. After all, white settlement began here.

The Clarence City Council at Rosny Park, off Bligh Street just north of the Eastlands shopping centre, has publications to direct you to scores of built reminders of the municipality's history. They include the nearby Rosny Historic Site featuring an old farm cottage, stone barn and a replica school. The Tasmanian Family History Society's library is in an old sandstone building in the main street of Bellerive, French for beautiful shore. The library has prodigious records of which Tasmanians came from where. Many a convict ancestor has been tracked down there. The building's Sound Museum is excellent.

A massive cannon six metres long and with a 203 mm bore at the old fort by the corner of aptly-named Fort and Gunning Streets at Kangaroo Point, Bellerive. Mounted in 1885, it weighs 26 tonnes and could fire projectiles weighing 82 kilograms. The gun was part of the defences for colonial Fortress Hobart.

Continue from the library to pretty Kangaroo Bluff with a host of gracious old residences. On top of the headland is the well pre-served former Bluff Battery, or fort of guns, built in 1885 in panic after the withdrawal of the Imperial garrisons to help protect Ho-bart and after two Russian gunboats entered the estuary in curious circumstances in 1873. About the same time the Alexandra Battery at lower Sandy Bay and the Domain Battery, where the war memo-rial Cenotaph is today, were commissioned, giving protection from invasion by sea. Community leaders spent their weekends in the Volunteer Artillery Corps training to defend Hobart against an en-emy that never came. The forts were decommissioned in the early 1900s.

Old Clarence Plains also has a lively history, laced with tales of bushrangers. The centrepiece of the popular Rokeby Historic Trail is St Matthews Anglican Church, built in 1843. Governor Arthur banished to this outpost the colony's first cleric, important diarist

and gregarious tippler with com-passion for convicts and Aborigi-nes, the Rev. Bobby Knopwood. He once owned Battery Point, acquired in part by Arthur to enhance the governor's fortune. Knopwood's grave is in the church grounds along with those of five from the First Fleet to arrive in Sydney in 1788.

The Risdon Cove site of Van Diemen's Land's first white settle-ment is seldom visited. As an act of reconciliation the State Gov-ernment in 1995 gave the area to the Aboriginal community. They welcome visitors to the site, off the B32 Derwent Highway. The area

The monument at Risdon Cove to mark the 100th anniversary of the landing by young John Bowen's intrepid pioneers in 1803.

has changed little since Bowen's brave but ill-fated landing there. Wild ducks, native hens and wallabies still thrive near a public bar-beque area by the reedy lagoon and the little stream that attracted the white pioneers. A big bluestone monument there commemo-rating the 100-year anniversary of their arrival was astonishingly contradicted by the State Government's ignoring of the 200th anni-versary. Instead, it celebrated in 2004 the second landing by Collins' party across the river five months later.

Risdon Cove, looking today much as it did at the time of the first white settlement.

PART EIGHT 190 km
The Huon, Bruny Island, New Norfolk
Plus a side trip to Franklin, Geeveston and Cockle Creek

A PRIME PART of our island is south of Hobart beside the superb D'Entrecasteaux Channel and through the Huon Valley. Add another day or more if you decide to go to Bruny Island and many other attractions including the Tahune AirWalk, Hastings Caves and on to Cockle Creek, the farthest south you can drive in Australia. Our Tour continues north from Hobart after this treat.

Take Sandy Bay Road south from the city, past Hobart's plushest suburbs and Wrest Point, near hundreds of moored pleasure craft. The cylindrical hotel was the first official legal casino in the nation. Its top-floor Revolving Restaurant has spectacular views of the whole city and the river. On the right, just past the Lower Sandy Bay shopping centre, are the impressive remains of the old Alexandra gun battery.

Sandy Bay Road at **Taroona** becomes the B68 Channel Highway, which mostly keeps the coast in sight. It is where you begin the Huon Trail, a tourist route teeming with old marvels and scores of places that make it a haven for foodies and wine buffs. Fruit from this district gave Tassie the moniker The Apple Isle. By 1827 almost every type of apple tree grown in England was thriving in Van Diemen's Land.

The sandstone Shot Tower along here was built in 1870. Your diligent authors have climbed the 259 steps to the top, from where molten lead was dropped into water to form gun shot. This process was almost obsolete at the time because of the arrival of the cased bullet, so it had a short career for its owner Joseph Moir.

Browns River, which you cross entering **Kingston**, was a tannin-coloured stream bordered by dense scrub, providing shellfish and crayfish for Aborigines until white settlers arrived in 1808. The

river is named after Scots surgeon-cum-botanist Robert Brown. He
visited the district in 1804 to add to his collection of 3,600 plant
specimens while spending more than three years travelling on *Investigator* with Matthew Flinders.

Check the directional signs. Have at least a look at Kingston
Beach, then join the B68 Channel Highway towards Blackmans Bay
and Margate. On your left near the second traffic roundabout out of
Kingston is the headquarters of the Australian Antarctic Division,
which runs the nation's activities in the great south land. They welcome visitors to a fascinating display of Antarctic memorabilia and

*The 1870 Shot Tower on the Huon Trail, Channel Highway. Molten
lead was dropped from the top of the tower into water to form gun
shot. Photo, Tony Hope..*

Sweeping Kingston Beach. Photo, Tony Hope.

(stuffed) animals, plus a reference library. The history of Antarctic exploration is illustrated graphically at the Islands to Ice display at the Tasmanian Museum and Art Gallery in Hobart.

Although our railway system never came to this part of the island the Margate Train complex just north of **Margate** has specialty shops and a restaurant in part of Tasmania's last passenger train, the Tasman Limited, beside an outstanding antiques shop. Your authors were regular travellers on the train, which ran between Hobart, Launceston and Stanley. A couple of kms on, left of the road just past the bridge over North West Bay River, is a solitary round rock as big as a truck. Notwithstanding stories about it being a meteorite among other things, the rock was spewed from a volcano many millions of years ago.

The story of Margate, based largely on timber-getting, seafaring and fruit growing, is well presented later on the Tour in the Channel Heritage Museum at our next stop, the village of **Snug**. The centre's displays cover the region from Margate south to Gordon. A re-created colonial home there has an interesting kitchen, bedroom, bathroom and washhouse. Along with outlying parts of Hobart, Snug was nearly wiped out by a raging bushfire in February 1967. 11 people were killed at Snug. While the fires still smouldered, Michael Tatlow walked down a street here where, remarkably, every brick home was rubble and timber homes were barely scorched. On the waterfront, next to the camping ground, is the official Tasmanian memorial park to these horrific bushfires that took 62 lives and destroyed 1,300 homes.

Pioneer explorers in about 1810 discovered and named the nearby river the Snug because it was a cosy place to anchor. Like so many places by the channel, Europeans' first sighting of Snug was in 1792, by France's Rear Admiral Bruni D'Entrecasteaux. Britain's Lieutenant John Hayes also mapped the channel a year later. Farther south is the village of **Kettering**, with an old hotel and a fine restaurant and gift shop beside hundreds of pleasure and fishing boats moored in Little Oyster Cove.

Bruny Island

KETTERING IS THE gateway to **Bruny Island**. Call at the local visitor information centre for directions, maps and brochures. A regular vehicular ferry service can take you to and from this wondrous island, which will take at least a few hours to explore.

The island has a long history, from the time Aborigines with bark canoes populated it perhaps 40,000 years ago. Your authors have explored a convict brickworks at Variety Bay on North Bruny of the mid 1800s. This was also a pilot station where fires were lit at night to guide ships from Storm Bay to the Derwent. Many of the bricks were used to build St Peter's Anglican Church here in 1847, now in ruins. In the early 1950s 20,000 unused bricks from here were used to build the Bligh Museum at Adventure Bay. We recommend a North Bruny circuit before going along the isthmus, with a fairy penguin rookery, to South Bruny.

Lovely **Adventure Bay** is indeed an historic place. It was a resting place for Captain William Bligh's ships. British Captain Tobias Furneaux, who sailed in company with Captain James Cook, named the bay after his ship in 1773. Cook's third visit here, with midshipman Matthew Flinders, was his last call in these waters before being killed in the Pacific Islands. Cook's Landing marks the great mariner's arrival here in 1788. The Bligh Museum of Pacific Exploration presents tales of intrepid seafarers who anchored in the bay. Bligh, a keen botanist, planted Tasmania's first apple trees here. He, like others, thought Bruny was part of mainland Van Diemen's

Land until Bruni D'Entrecasteaux sailed up the channel that has his name, as does the island. Look at the Wellington Range from here. It looks to have a flat top. So early sea explorers gave the outcrop its original name, Table Hill. Later namers dubbed it Mont du Plateau (d'Entrecasteaux), Skiddaw (Lt. Hayes), Table Mountain, Platform Mountain and Mount Collins (the Reverend Knopwood, after his Governor).

Drive across the island with wonderful views over Mount Mangana and some rain forest, despite blots of clear felling, to the settlement on the other side named **Lunawanna** after the tongue-twisting Aboriginal name for this island, Lunawannaalonnah. A drive of some 15 more kms takes you past eerie Cloudy Lagoon and the spectacular coastline of Cloudy Bay to the historic Cape Bruny lighthouse (1838) at the southern tip of the South Bruny National Park, overlooking the Great Southern Ocean. Allow an hour to drive back to the ferry past the island's "capital" **Alonnah**, plus half an hour for the Bruny Island Museum in the old Council Chambers.

CONTINUE SOUTH from Kettering on the B68 Channel Highway to the award-winning Peppermint Bay restaurant and hotel at **Woodbridge,** the destination for daily cruise trips on catamarans from Hobart. The road hugs the coast past **Middleton** and **Gordon** where there is a memorial to the French sea explorers, and then the holiday retreat of **Verona Sands**. Beyond little Huon Island and Garden Island, the Hartzview Vineyard and Wine Centre to the right off Woodbridge Hill Road at Gardners Bay has a

Fruit picking at the lush and lovely Hartzview Vineyard and Wine Centre with restaurant, built mid 1900s, off Woodbridge Road near Gardners Bay. Italian prisoners of war, in distinctive maroon clothes, where interned here during World War II.

nostalgic village of seven former fruit pickers' huts from the 1920s when families came to the Huon on annual working holidays. Follow the signs, up a bush road, to this scenic retreat, with a splendid restaurant, wines and a heritage b. & b. The huts are now listed on the heritage register. Italian prisoners of war were held here and at other places in the district as farm workers during World War II. They wore maroon clothes so the locals could identify them. Some liked the area so much they returned to the Huon to live.

Just along the B68 is romantic old **Cygnet**. Like so many towns of Tasmania, Cygnet (pop. 1,000) had earlier names. The first was Port des Cygnes (the port of swans) by Bruni d'Entrecasteaux. The town's estuary still has a healthy community of swans.

In the1850's the name was anglicised to Port Cygnet, followed by Lovett in 1862 after a local family, and finally Cygnet in 1915. The first European settler, William Nichols, arrived in 1834. Convict probation stations held hundreds of prisoners. Timber getting and milling and later coal mining were also important.

Cygnet is a fruit farming centre and home to many craftspeople, painters, musicians and retirees. Charles Wooley, familiar with most parts of the world, chose Cygnet as his family holiday retreat, at an upgraded former apple-packing shed.

Fanny Cochrane Smith, born on Flinders Island and a resident near here, claimed to be the last full-blood Tasmanian Aborigine, after Truganini died in Hobart in 1876. In the 1880s, an evidently-convinced Tasmanian Parliament granted Fanny a pension and about 1,000 hectares of land. Her recording in c.1903 of Aboriginal songs can be heard in the Aboriginal Gallery at the Tasmanian Museum.

A short drive through orchards and fields of sheep and cattle by the trout-rich Huon River takes you to **Huonville** (pop. 1,700). Bruni d'Entrecasteaux named the river and another than runs into it in honour of his Captain Huon de Kermandec. The general district became the Huon.

Huonville was first settled in 1839 by the Walton family. The only access to Hobart Town from the district for many years was by boat or on a rough bush track no cart could cover. A contemporary scribe said that with the coming of horseless carriages, "The time is not far distant when motor vehicles will take all the animation and romance out of the 'tooling' of coaches on this road." The cover of this book shows a party of such coach travellers heading for Huonville.

Bright Star was one of many brands of apples from the vast orchards of the Huon, making the State The Apple Isle.

RIGHT: Tulips, many of them exported to Holland, are among the scores of crops farmed in the Huon.

The Huon Valley Apple and Heritage Museum is at **Grove** just north of the town. The local Visitor Information Centre beside the Huon River can direct you to places like heritage-listed Matilda's of **Ranelagh** with an oast house in the grounds. Queen Elizabeth II once visited the place. By apple orchards, grape vines, a dairy farm and forested slopes also at Ranelagh is the Home Hill Winery Restaurant, well known to your authors.

The first cars cross the new bridge over the Huon River at Huonville in the 1920s.
Colin Dennison Collection.

✳✳✳

YOU CAN NOW return to Hobart in a casual 40 minutes taking the A6 Huon Highway or the B64, the more-scenic old highway by the mountain. The Wellington mountain range on the left from the highway features Sleeping Beauty. Its skyline, lonely timber-getting pioneers reckoned, looked like a long-haired woman's breasts and other things. If you have a few more hours, though, cross the river at Huonville and go on south, visiting the Tahune AirWalk, Hastings Caves and some fascinating old towns to the most southerly settlement in Australia.

SIDE TRIP

Franklin, Port Huon, Geeveston, Cockle Creek

Franklin (pop. 500) beside the Huon River was once the biggest town in the district. The name comes from colourful Lady Franklin, wife of Lieut. Governor Sir John Franklin who later died trying to find a North West Passage north of Canada. She bought land here in 1838, sub-divided it and sold her holding -- on the condition that its new owners were strictly religious. Quite a demand, that was, in those grog-sodden days. Still, a temperance society was formed and the locality became known as Teetotal Valley.

The Franklin Wooden Boat Centre here shows off fine boats made from unique Tasmanian timbers and has records of the past building of many magnificent craft.

A Hereford bull rests beside a Huon farmhouse that has seen better days. Photo, Charles Wooley.

Continue south beside the river on the Huon Highway past Shipwrights Point and the old apple shipping wharf to idyllic **Port Huon**, a great spot for sailors by the mouth of the Kermandie River. Do visit the gracious Kermandie Hotel here facing the waterfront where there will soon be a substantial marina.

Geeveston (pop. 850), farther south, is named after farmer and clergyman William Geeves, who in 1842 arrived at Hobart Town from England. Soon after, he answered a call for a bush preacher to go here.

Stately old St James church at Ranelagh, north-west of Huonville. Photo, Tony Hope.

His family planted the area's first apple trees. They lived in slab huts when supplies came by river boats.

Timber miller Richard Hill migrated to Tasmania in 1853 to set up the Liverpool and Honeywood Tramway Company to cart timber and provisions locally. William Geeves and brother John had 108 grandchildren. A Geeves family reunion in 1992 recorded that William and John had 6,636 direct descendants. There would be more than 10,000 of them now. The Geeveston Forest and Heritage Centre presents with flair the district's forest-related culture.

If you fancy a stroll on a swinging walkway high over the forest and Huon River, take a 28-km drive from Geeveston through luxuriant bushland to Forestry Tasmania's Tahune Forest AirWalk. A cantilevered section of the AirWalk extends 48 metres above the Huon, just below its confluence with the Picton River. The Hartz Mountains, in the national park of that name and to which you can drive, loom in the south. You can also see Huon pines growing on a 20-minute walk from the visitors' centre.

The Huon Highway continues south from Geeveston through **Dover** at Port Esperance, where Henry Jones and Co. once had a dried fruit and fruit pulp factory, to the fishing and farming centre of **Southport**. From here you can visit wondrous dolomite Hastings Caves and take a dip in the pool of warm thermal spring water. There are guided tours in Newdegate Cave, which has vast chambers. It is claimed to be the largest cave open to tourists in Australia. Like scores of Tasmanian places, the cave was named after a State Governor. Then go for a ride on the historic Ida Bay railway, built in the 1890s for lugging timber and later coal and lime.

You might decide to go farther south along a gravel road to beautiful, unsullied Recherché Bay, where D'Entrecasteaux spent some time in 1793. It is much the same as the French explorers saw it over 200 years ago. At the southern end is **Cockle Creek,** a coal mining settlement from the 1840's and now a coastal holiday resort and a starting point for walkers to the southern tip of Tasmania. The 19 km journey from Dover takes you as far south as possible by road in Australia. The main roads through Huonville will get you back to Hobart in a couple of hours.

✳✳✳

OUR TOUR continues north from Hobart on the A1 Brooker Highway from the traffic roundabout beside the Queens Domain.

A pleasant drive through the city's northern suburbs takes you to the **Bridgewater** bridge over the Derwent. This place was called Green Point until 1829, when convicts

The brilliant Forestry Tasmania AirWalk over the Huon River at Tahune, west of Geeveston.

began building a causeway near where Austins Ferry was the vital link with the colony's midlands and north. They quarried and carted stone, and sank it in the mud, often labouring chest-deep in stinking slime. Most of them were in leg irons and slept in cells less than a metre high. A bridge spanning the Derwent, linking the sundered ends of the island, opened to coaches in 1849. The Old Watch House at the beginning of the causeway is a relic of this activity.

Along the way to Bridgewater, colonial coach travellers took a drink at the infamous Green Man Inn. A police officer went there disguised as a civilian traveller to get evidence of shady dealings by the inn-keeper, including peddling sly grog. The spy, foolish fellow, bedded and confided in the barmaid. The spy vanished after she betrayed him to the boss. The policeman's skeleton was found down the inn's 15-metre well, after 30 years of everyone (except the inn-keeper) drawing drinking water from it.

The Derwent curves down from New Norfolk in the Valley of Love. Photo, Tony Hope.

Do not cross the Bridgewater bridge. Our Tour goes that way later. Go straight ahead from the highway just before the bridge to follow the Derwent on the A10 Lyell Highway for a scenic 17-km ride to **New Norfolk.** This beautiful town (pop. 7,000) straddling a broad stretch of the river is a fine place to spend a day or three.

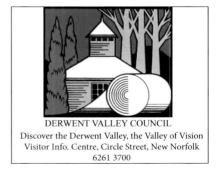

DERWENT VALLEY COUNCIL
Discover the Derwent Valley, the Valley of Vision
Visitor Info. Centre, Circle Street, New Norfolk
6261 3700

The romantic vale is known as the Valley of Love. The East India Company's Lieutenant John Hayes was the first European here, on a boating expedition in the wilds in 1793. Europeans settled here in 1806. They engaged pretty well with the local Aborigines.

Elegant old Tynwald by the river at New Norfolk. Now an outstanding b. & b., it was modernised in the 1890s.

It was named The Hills when the hamlet's size leaped dramatically over a few years from 1808 with the arrival of hundreds of free settlers who had reluctantly left their homes and farms on the South Pacific's Norfolk Island. That island, not *this* island, was the second colony

Looking south to the ruins of the Lachlan River flour mill, which operated at Tynwald from 1819.

of organised white settlement in Australia, from 1788. After 19 years of white settlement, the English Colonial Office decided Norfolk Island was not viable and ordered the Norfolk Evacuation to Van Diemen's Land. Norfolk Island later became a brutal place of punishment for convicts, administered from Tasmania in the 1840s.

Nine sailings delivered some 750 free settlers and convicts to Tasmania, nearly doubling the colony's population. With more than half of the settlers sailing on to The Hills, it inevitably became New Norfolk.

But Governor Macquarie from Sydney went up the river on a barge in 1811 and reckoned this bonny settlement should become a significant town, perhaps the capital of the island. Ignoring the settlement's proclamation as New Norfolk three years earlier, he blithely renamed the district Macquarie, and the village Elizabeth Town "in honour of my dear good wife and I have christened the rivulet the Thames"! Wife Elizabeth was with him. Some people claim he was renaming the Derwent but Macquarie's journal proves that the governor's Thames flows into the Derwent by the village.

Hop picking was a family affair in the Derwent Valley in the 1920s. Colin Dennison Collection.

The governor still called the village Elizabeth Town when he returned in 1821. This time the Macquaries brought their young son, named Lachlan, which was also the governor's first name. To leave his child's mark on the town along with his and his wife's, Macquarie changed the name of the rivulet, which he had called the Thames, to Lachlan's River. The people of New Norfolk would not cop the governor's indulgent moniker for their settlement.

Fruit orchards, then hops for the world's beer brewers, were planted in rich alluvial soil by the Derwent. The first hop plants were brought from Kent by William Shoobridge in 1822. They thrived to establish the cradle of Australia's hop industry. Bushy Park Estates just south of the village of Bushy Park, north of New Norfolk, is one of many captivating old hop-growing properties near the river.

Incidentally, your authors have learned that hop vines are sexy numbers. Before hop harvesting time, a lot of the vines droop at the top. The others are alertly erect. These are the males.

The town's attractions include the Old Colony Inn, the Oast House Hop Industry Museum, the now-deserted asylum at Willow Court and fishing and boating.

Enjoy a drink and a meal at the Bush Inn by the river in Montagu Street. It is probably Australia's oldest continuously-open hotel, licensed in 1815. The view over the Derwent from the hotel inspired visiting Irish composer William Vincent Wallace to write an aria for the wonderful opera *Maritana*, first performed in London in 1843. Wallace said at the time, "Tasmania is a place where beauty has made her home". Dame Nellie Melba sang songs from the opera at the Bush Inn in 1924 and the ABC presented a pioneering broadcast of it, transmitted live to Hobart.

The district saw a famous gun battle at the time Wallace was composing. Police took on "gentleman bushranger" Martin Cash with Lawrence Cavenagh, George Jones and others, who hung out at what is now called Cash's Cave in a forested valley feeding Cash's Creek at Magra, across the Derwent. This was in February 1843, two months after the three escaped dramatically from Port Arthur and just after they bailed up 16 people at the fine Stanton homestead at Magra. Cash, Cavenagh and Jones, however, got away unscathed. The residence was built by convicts for a former convict in 1817. It is now a superior b. & b. centre, with colonial furnishings, on Back River Road.

The original Willow Court complex was apparently built in 1830 to an Indian Army design as a soldiers' barracks and convict asylum on orders of Lieut. Governor Arthur. Around it grew Australia's largest asylum, with 1,000 patients. It closed in 2001 and only a remnant of its formidable buildings is left. Michael Tatlow remembers seeing as a child a sign over the entrance through high walls: Lunatic Asylum. The soldiers introduced horse racing and Freemasonry to the colony.

Sublimely sited by the bridge over the Derwent, 1825 Woodbridge b. & b. and former gentleman's residence has a convict cellar.

North of the Derwent is the 1856 grave of who we are assured was the first white woman to step on land in Australia. She was Betty King, a free woman in New Norfolk after being a convict with the First Fleet in Sydney in 1788. Her simply-engraved tombstone is in a church cemetery on Lawitta Road, Lawitta, off Hamilton Road. She was 93.

New Norfolk has an abundance of colonial accommodation. Two examples are Woodbridge and Tynwald. Elegant Tynwald was once a typical square-fronted Georgian home, substantially "modernised" in the 1890s to its present grand Victorian appearance by Manxman, the Hon. William Moore MLC. The ruins of the Lachlan River flour mill, built by convicts for original owner John Terry in 1819, are in front of the house. The mill is depicted in a magnificent stained glass window in the town's St Matthews Anglican Church. Opened in 1824, it is the oldest church in Tasmania, we're told, but little remains of the original building.

Your authors have enjoyed staying at Woodbridge on the Derwent, sublimely placed on the southern bank of the river beside the bridge. The restored "gentleman's residence" built in 1825 was the largest house in the district. Its cost of a thousand pounds was considered amazingly high. A lockup where convicts were shackled is downstairs. Looking at the river from around Woodbridge, with trout and swallows chasing insects, it is easy to imagine the river steamers and sail boats that plied between here and Hobart. There is a lot to see and do in old New Norfolk.

Stanton, a marvellous 1817 home, now a superior b. & b. with colonial furnishings, at Magra. A garden party there was raided by Martin Cash and his bushranging gang.

The 1815 Bush Inn, probably Australia's oldest continuously-open hotel, where a famous opera aria was composed and later sung there by Dame Nellie Melba.

Our naughty governors

WE MUST NOTE that atop a hill as you drive into New Norfolk was a colonial house of vice-regal debauchery.

Now Turriff Lodge, the 1815 Government Cottage and farm, now gone, was a country retreat for governors from the duties of state. And in the mid 1840s it was the centre of tales of licentious dalliance by old Lieut. Governor Sir John Eardley-Wilmot, who had sired 12 children and whose second wife remained in England.

Eardley-Wilmot enjoyed the company of younger women. He regularly and openly coached to Government Cottage for weekends of alleged wickedness with acclaimed beauty, Julia Sorell, granddaughter of Lieut. Governor Sorell. Society of bawdy Van Diemen's Land was scandalised, leading to Eardley-Wilmot's sacking from London in 1846, a year before he died in Hobart. Governor Sorell himself had a "Mrs Sorell", who was the wife of an officer.

The colony's first Lieut. Governor Collins, it seems, played around, too. He left behind in England his wife, who had a daughter. He had two children with a mistress in Sydney. Then in Hobart another child to his mistress, Margaret Eddington, who had a convict husband. There is no record of this causing dismay but a later governor or two were sent packing for misconduct.

PART NINE 160 km
Derwent Valley, Pontville, Oatlands, Ross

Plus a side trip to Mt Field National Park, the Valley of the Giants & Lake Pedder

WE RECOMMEND spending at least a few hours up the sublime Derwent Valley north of New Norfolk on the western side of the Derwent and see the beautiful old Salmon Ponds trout farm at **Plenty**. You can feed giant fish and dine here. In 1864 this tranquil place became the first trout hatchery in the southern hemisphere and looks much as it did then.

The museum tells the heroic story of sailing clippers bringing Atlantic salmon and trout eggs from England and the releasing of trout throughout the island, sometimes by fishing visionaries riding horses to alpine tarns. The Salmon Ponds' promoters wanted to establish an Atlantic salmon industry and the introduction of English trout was a secondary consideration. After a couple of failures, young salmon were released to follow the Derwent to the sea. There they were expected to complete their life cycle by returning to their place of origin to spawn as they do in the northern hemisphere.

Pioneer hops grower William Shoobridge's magnificent oast house beside a duck pond at Bushy Park.

To everyone's dismay, they never came back. But the trout thrived. Atlantic salmon are today farmed in nets in several parts of the island but have never acclimatised.

Continue through grazing and hop fields sheltered by protecting poplars that turn gold in autumn at **Bushy Park** and **Glenora** to **Westerway** beside the Tyenna River. Many early oast houses, where the hops were dried, dot the landscape.

Better than returning now to New Norfolk, take half a day by turning left at Westerway to follow the Tyenna on the B61 Gordon River Road to the extensive Something Wild Wildlife Sanctuary and the Mt Field National Park, Tasmania's original such park, with its impressive Russell Falls.

Charlie Wooley by a fallen giant at Mt Field National Park. Photo Donna Sookee.

Then, for the highlight of the whole Tasmanian tour for many, visit in the Styx River valley to stroll in nature's cathedral among the tallest hardwood trees in the world. The Valley of the Giants is a non-commercialised wonder, so take your own refreshments.

To get there, turn right 2.5 km beyond the old forestry village of **Maydena**, onto the Florentine Road. Take the first turn to the right again to the Styx Road, through the underpass. Have a contemplative stop at the bridge over the Styx River where it joins with the South Styx.

The stream that divides this wild (now tarnished) paradise is named after a river of Greek mythology that flows to hell and divides the world of the living from the world of the dead. From paradise, we prefer to think. But actually, pioneers who found the river lined by tall trees and clogged with fallen logs after a flood named it The Sticks. Later arrivals, perhaps on hearing the name but not the spelling, endowed it with its hellish name of today.

There was plenty of room for 18 people on the cut trunk of this eucalypt in the Styx Valley. Photo courtesy The Wilderness Society.

The once-pristine forests here, you will see, show the aftermath of logging and the burning of remaining vegetation. 6 km from the underpass are regimented rows of one-species plantation replacements. Wildlife is scarce around here, where carrots laced with 1080 poison were spread to wipe out animals that might chomp on plantation shoots.

Continue to the Big Tree reserve, a patch of protected swamp gums (eucalyptus regnans), some of which were growing when Tasman, the discoverer of Tasmania in 1642, was a lad. A boardwalk with interpretation boards, thanks to Forestry Tasmania, takes you through this sublime cathedral of trees 95 metres high, with bases five metres wide. Yes, the tallest hardwoods in the world; higher than the highest peak of the Sydney Opera House. These are historic icons that should be revered at least as much as man-made structures.

A short track from the road opposite the boardwalk goes through native forest to the gurgling Styx River. There are lots of loggers' roads (some locked off) around here and it is easy to get lost, so take care. Return to the Gordon River Road the same way you came here.

Ideally, go for a further hour or two of casual motoring beyond Maydena to eye-boggling Lakes Pedder and Gordon at the edge of Tasmania's South West Wilderness. The flooding of the smaller and ancient Lake Pedder for power generation outraged many people around 1972. Two activists were allegedly murdered when their light aircraft, perhaps sabotaged, vanished as it took them to Canberra to argue their case.

Today's huge lakes provide good fishing in spectacular wild country. The former hydro-electricity workers' village of **Strathgordon** has a hotel and the Gordon Dam information centre.

Pioneer photographer Olegas Truchanas' superb picture of the natural Lake Pedder before it was flooded in 1972, visited years earlier by Mike Tatlow. Beaches have re-established, however.

IF YOU HAVE taken the side trip, return to New Norfolk and cross the bridge over the Derwent there to continue the Grand Tour. Turn right along the river's northern shore on the B10 road, overlooking the river and farms.

The two-humped outcrop to the north is Mt Dromedary on top of which bushrangers Cash, Kavanagh and Jones had their "fortress" in 1843. The road takes you to the dormitory town of **Bridgewater**. Turn left and motor north on the A1. This historic road linking Hobart and Launceston is officially the Midland Highway but tourism-conscious entrepreneurs have dubbed it the Heritage Highway. A wealth of early buildings and villages line this route.

Most of the midlands was lightly timbered with many open plains. For thousands of years they were Aboriginal hunting grounds. But from about 1810 most of the grazing land was granted to free settlers with money and a generous supply of convict labour to establish farms with often grand houses in less than 30 years.

Construction of the road, from the north and south, began in 1820 after James Meehan surveyed the route in 1812. Any day from 1830 to 1840, a thousand convicts in gangs with crude tools built and improved the road and many bridges. It has been rerouted here and there over the years, recently bypassing most of the impressive old villages that we explorers must see. So, don't take the bypasses.

From 1816, before coaches, the mail was delivered by lone horsemen, some of them trusted convicts toting muskets to repel bushrangers and, sometimes, hostile natives. The journey between Hobart and Launceston took several days by horse and coach, with overnight accommodation and fresh horses provided at several inns. By 1840 the road between the two cities, still with a ferry to cross the Derwent, was a little more than today's 200 km. Coaches drawn by four or six horses were able to complete the journey in two days by the mid 1850s. Today the trip from city to city takes two-and-a-half hours, if you're in a hurry.

Highwaymen regularly robbed coaches and their passengers. It seems, though, that many of the colonial highwaymen were a gallant lot. They took money, food and clothes but, on our evidence, generally treated ladies respectfully. They did not slay their victims unless threatened. Not that that saved scores of highwaymen from being hanged.

The next town, **Brighton**, was named by Governor Macquarie in 1821 after "our present gracious Sovereign's favourite place of residence". It became a major military training camp in the early and mid 1900s, then a settlement camp for European immigrants who had fled the ravages of World War II. Get directions to nearby splendid Bonorong Wildlife Park to the right of the highway in Brighton for close-up encounters with Tasmanian native animals.

The intriguing old village of **Pontville** is on a hilly section of the highway at the Jordan River. It developed as an extension of Brighton in the 1840s. The district was first settled about 1810.

Before then it was, by repute, a favourite spot for soldiers with convicts and dogs hunting kangaroos and Tasmanian emus to help feed hungry Hobart Town, which endured months without a visit by a supply ship from Sydney.

One of the hunters, a private in the Royal Marines named Hugh Germaine, perhaps gave biblical names to places around here. He claimed to have named Bagdad, Jericho, Jerusalem (now Colebrook), the Jordan River and Lake Tiberius. Private Hugh, we understand, carried a bible and the *Arabian Nights* in his saddlebag. The namers, though, may have been surveyors. See silhouette No. 7 on page 143.

Pontville was a garrison town in the mid 1800s. The barracks, now Lythgow's Row accommodation centre, is on the right next to the bridge. The town prospered as a rural centre and changing station for coach horses going to and from Hobart Town. The population reached 2,000 in the 1860s when the town had six flour mills. The municipality of Brighton was named in 1863. Your authors often take a break at the town's Crown Inn Hotel (c. 1835), once a colonial ale-house.

The splendid little stone church on the right near the top of the hill as you leave Pontville is Romanesque Saxon style St Marks Church of England, built between 1839 and 1841 and designed by the talented convict James Blackburn. Look out to the left for the white Cornish-style cottage (1820s), huge Wybra Hall (early 1900s) and four other fine old residences along the Heritage Mile at **Mangalore**, five minutes drive north.

Bagdad, a few kms up the highway, was settled in 1813. It became another horse-changing station, or stage, before north-bound coaches tackled Constitution Hill, a steep climb at the time that called for a pretty good constitution. But the name comes from the gentle rise near Buckingham Palace, London.

On the right is the fading sign over a former butcher's shop. The Bagdad butcher was on the receiving end of a lot of jokes world-wide in the late 1990s when Saddam Hussein of Iraq was called the Butcher of Baghdad. Sadly, the shop then closed.

Beyond Constitution Hill is old **Kempton**. Europeans first settled here in 1814. The village was founded in 1838, named Kemp Town after Captain Antony Fenn Kemp who was granted a lot of land in the then Green Ponds area. He opened a shop in Sydney before coming to Van Diemen's Land as second in command to Launceston's founder, Colonel Paterson, in 1804. Kemp was quite a rogue, a merchant and a banker on the island. His old homestead is Mount Vernon, named after George Washington's mansion in Virginia. It is well preserved today. Kemp died, grumpily, aged 94 in 1868. Kempton had seven taverns in its heyday and was the centre of a rich grazing area.

Impressively-restored Dysart House, built at Kempton in 1842.

The sandstone mansion on the right driving into Kempton is Dysart House. Master stonemason Andrew Bell built it from 1842 to 1845 for William Ellis as the Green Ponds Hotel, probably the most imposing coaching inn then on the road to Launceston. Ellis was a prospering pardoned convict, transported from England for embezzlement. Dysart House's current owner, social commentator Leo Schofield, has restored his home superbly and opens it to the public several times a year.

Murderous bushranger Matthew Brady, who has "lookouts" named after him at several locations, loved to ridicule his pursuers. He turned the tables on Lieut. Governor Arthur in 1825 when Brady nailed on the door of Kempton's then Royal Oak Hotel a reward poster offering 20 gallons of rum to anyone who delivered the governor to him.

The fox hunt, a precious sport with hounds and traditional English trappings, was popular here at Tedworth and other Midlands properties in the 1800s. Introduced foxes, however, were soon eradicated by devils and the hunters.

The highway's silhouettes

SOME 200 METRES south of the old **Melton Mowbray** Hotel, left beside the highway, is a marvellous, black steel-plate silhouette of a police sergeant taking a bottle-toting drunk to jail in a wheelbarrow. This records a real colonial event and is the most southerly of 12 such depictions of history along the highway.

They are at your left and right for 50 km. Some are easy to miss, so we present here a cheater's guide to their locations. The last is near Tunbridge.

The entertaining pieces are the idea and designs of sculptors Maureen Craig and Folko Kooper. They created the project as a gift to the local communities at their 1830s home and studio at Georgian Oakwood, one of the Heritage Mile buildings back at Mangalore. Local councils installed the silhouettes, mostly on disused sections of the old Hobart Road. See, in order:

2.   Precisely six kms north of Melton Mowbray, on the left just past the 1820s Lovely Banks homestead, once a convict probation station, and near a convict-built sandstone bridge, a horseman, his bag flying in the wind, gallops the mail to Launceston.

3.   The next silhouette is 5.5 kms on, to the left past Spring Hill, the highest rise on the highway, named from a spring there that filled a horse trough. It shows Samuel Page's premier coach drawn by four horses speeding north on a section of the original road. Samuel's remains are under a monument in the Oatlands cemetery.

4.   3.5 kms along on a rise at your right, is a shepherd with his flock, recalling this wool district's past when boundary fences were rare.

5.   4.3 kms on, past the exit road from Jericho, and easy to miss in a paddock to your left, the figure trudging south with his staff and bag depicts the infamous Solomon Blay. He was the southern colonial hangman, who lived at Oatlands. Blay usually had to walk to work at the jail in Hobart Town. He could not afford a horse and few would provide a ride to this man who reeked of death; the executor of at least 200 men and women.

6.   Just 2.2 kms along in a hilly field on the left, perhaps extinct Tasmanian Tigers (or thylacines) roam where they were once fairly common. The colonial government paid a bounty for heads of the tigers, often wrongly blamed for killing sheep.

7.   3.5 kms north, the two figures well apart on the left taking theodolite readings immortalise the surveyors for the highway. Some reports say these men (not Private Hugh Germaine, recorded at Pontville) were the bible carriers who named Jericho, Bagdad, Jerusalem, Lake Tiberius and the Jordon River.

8.   Exactly one km on is the top of Lemon Hill. It is named after the colony's first significant bushranger, the evil Richard Lemon. He is depicted on your left bailing up a horseman, whom he probably shot dead, not necessarily here and long before the road was built. A convict with a ticket-of-leave, Lemon scarp-

3. Samuel Page's coach, Launceston bound.

A drunk at Melton Mowbray off to the lock-up.

2. A colonial mailman.

5. Solomon Blay, hangman. Some wit gave him a Santa hat.

ered from a farm in 1806. Two Irish escapees who joined him annoyed the Englishman by speaking Irish. So Lemon shot one of them and hung the body upside down from a tree. Lemon murdered at least three soldiers in a two-year spree before farmer Michael Mansfield posed as a fellow fleeing felon, got Lemon drunk with two bottles of rum and shot him dead. Mansfield and confederates took Lemon's head to Hobart Town and collected a then-princely reward of 50 pounds. The head was planted on a stake on March 1, 1808, and displayed for all to see in Hobart to prove that the brute bushranged no longer. Nonetheless, Lemon Springs and Lemon's Lagoon (now Lake Tiberius near Stonor, where Lemon had a hut) were also named after him.

8. Evil bushranger Richard Lemon bails up a traveller.

10. Soldiers, who guarded convicts and hunted crooks.

9. Off to church?

12. Tasmanian emus, killed off for eating.

11. The protective sheep would not leave these convict road builders when we were there.

9. Exactly two kms north on your right, also on the old Hobart Road, is the folksy silhouette of a man with his horse and cart. He is in his Sunday best duds going to church.

10. Past Oatlands, on the right 6.5 km from the Sunday man, is a troop of marching colonial soldiers with muskets. The military controlled the convicts who built this road. They also hunted bushrangers and Aborigines who sometimes raided farmsteads.

11. Also on the right, 2.6 km on, are three convict road builders. This was a difficult section of their work, with engineering obstacles.

12. Don't miss the stark silhouettes of two Tasmanian emus on the top of a rise about 50 metres to your right 14.1 km north of the convicts. Smaller than mainland Australian emus, the last of them was shot before 1850. This is the last of Maureen's and Folko's creations. May there be many more!

CONTINUING OUR GRAND TOUR north of Melton Mowbray, look for the sign on the left to take the old Hobart road through bypassed **Jericho** with many old farm buildings.

Rose Cottage, of bright orange bricks made by convicts in 1823, is at the hamlet's southern end. Known formerly as Blacksmiths Cottage and Forge Cottage, it was sadly decaying when we were there. But a new owner is restoring Rose Cottage to its colonial richness.

Rose Cottage, a notable 1823 Georgian house of convict-made bricks of orange at Jericho. Photo, Tony Hope.

The iconic 1836 Callington Mill at Oatlands.

Going, going ... Sheep market day 1930s in the Midlands. Colin Dennison Collection

In the 1830s, this was the entrance to the Oatlands jail.

On the right opposite a former military commandant's residence are the remnants of the Mud Walls, a convict probation station (1841-48) made of mud bricks. Plaques there will tell you about it.

Gloriously-intact old **Oatlands'** fascinating history is illustrated by its many fine stone buildings. Take a walk along the main and side streets to marvel, as if you have time-travelled, at Georgian cottages, inns, churches, the 1829 court house, the old jail entrance and the Callington windmill. Oatlands also has some of the best examples of early dry-stone fences in the nation. Get directions from the visitor information centre in the main street and visit the Historical Society's rooms.

Governor Macquarie passed through here in 1811 and 1821. It was called Great Lagoon until he renamed the town on his second visit. Not because oats were grown here, incidentally. In typical fashion, Macquarie dubbed it after Oatlands, the English country seat of the then Duke of York, who appointed Macquarie Governor of NSW.

On his first trip on the road to Launceston the egotistical governor named Macquarie Point and two places south of here where he camped overnight Governor Macquarie's Resting Place and "Macquarie Springs or Governor's Second Resting Place". Mercifully, those names met public distain and died.

Surveying for Oatlands and its proposed 80 km of streets began in 1832. It was one of four military outposts along the road to Launceston. The others were at Brighton, Campbell Town and Perth. The first regiment in Oatlands put up their tents near the shore of Lake Dulverton, of 283 hectares when (sadly seldom) full.

The landmark Callington flour mill operated from 1837 to 1892. It is the third oldest windmill in Australia. It was gutted by fire early last century and left an empty shell for many years. Thanks to Bicentennial funding, it and its outbuildings with old farm machinery are major local attractions. As we write, the mill is being restored to its original working order to grind flour for tourist sale on the spot.

North of Oatlands is St Peter's Pass, considered a risky place in the days of bushrangers. Shrubs beside the highway here have been cleverly clipped in the shape of animals. A main roads employee began the tradition of this entertaining topiary in the mid 1960s. On the right further on, at Antill Ponds, are the ruins of the one-time best known of all the Midland roadside pubs, the celebrated Half Way House Hotel. Its doors closed for the last time in the late 1940s.

Farther on, also-bypassed **Tunbridge** is a tiny shadow of the Tunbridge Wells Inn which immigrant Thomas Wells named after the town in England. It was a major coach-staging place, pretty well half way between Hobart and Launceston. Until 50 years ago, the de-licensed Tun-

A reindeer shrub in St Peters Pass.

bridge Hotel was a favourite midway meal stopover for travellers. The Blackman's River bridge here is the oldest single-span timber bridge in Australia. Legend says it got that name after natives, in 1820, speared two herdsmen who were buried nearby.

For a taste of colonial life on a farm, follow the signed road on the right some nine km north of Tunbridge to the Somercotes property. You can buy succulent cherries and a snack in its Ticket-of-Leave building in summer and stay in nearby colonial cottages. The property near the Macquarie River is home to a flock of free-ranging turkeys. It has an intact old blacksmith's shop, a double-thatched dairy, a gathering of old farm implements and a glorious old homestead. British merchant navy captain Samuel Horton left the China seas to settle at Somercotes in 1823. The sixth generation of his family, the Riggalls (from Horton's sister Jane and William Riggall), still runs the property. Captain Horton was a pillar of a once-strong Methodist community around here. In the late 1800s, a renowned Methodist boys' boarding school, Horton College, flourished opposite Somercotes.

SNAPSHOT 1843
The day bushrangers hit Somercotes

FROST STILL WHITENED the shaded side of the trees and buildings as three men on horses, after some skirmishing, herded 15 farm workers and servant women into the courtyard beside the homestead at the Somercotes farm late one June morning in 1843.

The horsemen had gathered the workers at gun- and bayonet-point from the fields and outbuildings as hostages so they could not flee to alert the constables at Ross. The raiders were intent on robbing the property of money,

The turkey tree. Four turkeys were still perched in their overnight tree when we first visited Somercotes.

grog, food and weapons to take to their hideout in the hills.

They were convicts who had escaped dramatically by swimming across what they believed was a shark infested bay from the penal station a few days ride south at Port Arthur. They had raided a score of properties and stage-coaches, sometimes engaging in gun fights, in the six months since that rare escape in the dark.

"No one move!" their leader pleasantly told the gathering in a thick Irish brogue. He was a giant of a man with shoulder-length carroty hair and holding a musket with a bayonet. He also carried a big revolver. Some of the workers nodded and smiled, feeling a sort of kinship. They were Ticket-of-Leave convicts, hoping to receive pardons from mostly-minor thievery convictions that had resulted in their banishment from Ireland and England to this isle in the antipodes. One of the convicts gladly led the raiders to the homestead.

The big man was charismatic Martin Cash, aged 33, transported to Van Diemen's Land as a teenager for house-breaking and then given a second sentence of seven years for stealing six eggs. Many people by then called him the Robin Hood of the island; a robber of only the rich and gallant towards women. He was the colony's most wanted felon. Parties of soldiers were posted about the colony hoping to catch him. Cash dismounted and turned to his accomplices. They were Lawrence Cavenagh, aged 38, transported for life for burglary in Dublin, and another "lifer" George Jones, once a highwayman in Surrey, England.

"Lawrence, guard our friends," Cash instructed. He motioned to Jones. "Come with me."

Instead, Jones charged ahead for the homestead, where their booty awaited. But the robbers realised now that they were confronting a fortress. The rear cobblestone courtyard was secured by heavy gates and high walls of sandstone topped by an iron palisade with spikes 16 cm long. They were angled outwards and upwards to deter the likes of Cash & co. Iron bars and cedar shutters covered all the windows of the gracious residence of stone blocks. Iron bars protected the external doorways.

Jones amazingly scaled the wall, as a scout rushed inside to alert Captain Horton. Cash followed, clambering over a convict who had been induced to climb up and lay over part of the rampart. Horton rushed outside. He fought the two before he was beaten to the ground. Aged 38, he had built the residence just two years before.

Expecting more defenders to be inside, Cash fired a musket shot through the back doorway. It ricocheted along the hall, imbedding in the timber architrave by the front door.

Charlie Wooley briefly considers scaling Somercotes' spiked palisade, built to deter raiders.

As Jones guarded Horton and a few servants, Cash stormed inside. He pounded the barrel of his blunderbuss on the locked door to the room where he reckoned Horton's wife Elizabeth was trapped. On entering, an open window told him she had escaped, probably to run or ride about two kilometres to Ross for help.

Cash & co. knew they must also flee. They rode off with a load of grog and food, waving to a defiant Horton and his workers; the residence left undamaged and the farm animals untouched as a murder of crows squawked from the trees.

Cash's bullet is still in the architrave and the dents from his gun barrel are in the door. Bushranger George Jones was hanged for mur-

der from the busy gallows in Hobart 10 months after robbing Somercotes. Lawrence Cavanagh, driven mad at the jail on Norfolk Island, was hanged for murder with 13 others in 1846. Just before the execution, he was allowed a yarn with his old mate and fellow prisoner, Martin Cash.

Despite a conviction for murder, Cash married fellow convict Mary Bennett on Norfolk Island and ended his days a free and contented man at his little apple orchard at Glenorchy, Hobart, aged 69. It was in 1877, year the Port Arthur prison closed. Cash also became a caretaker at Hobart's Government House gardens.

CROSS THE FAMOUS bridge over the Macquarie River and stand by the war memorial at the main intersection in **Ross**. Look in any direction to see the pretty-well intact gracious country town of 150 years ago. The Macquarie meanders north through mostly farmland from Tooms Lake, past Cressy to Longford, where it joins the mightier South Esk River.

Fly fisher Tatlow amusing the trout where the historic bridge crosses the Macquarie River at picturesque Ross.

Governor Macquarie named the village in 1821 after the home seat of a mate in Scotland. The pride here is the remarkable bridge of carved stone designed by John Lee Archer, built by convicts and opened in 1836. The enigmatic carvings are attributed to talented convict stonemason Daniel Herbert. Built by using the same technology as the Romans 2,000 years ago, the ornate bridge would be considered a masterpiece anywhere in the world.

Convicts who reckoned they deserved a break from bridge work one Christmas Day slipped off to the nearby Man o' Ross tavern but the drinks they had were costly. The merry men were arrested, flogged and imprisoned at Port Arthur.

Ross is in the heart of Australia's super-fine wool industry. The Tasmanian Wool Centre showing off the district's woolly heritage and the celebrated old Man o' Ross Hotel are near the town square in elm-tree-lined Church Street going north to rejoin the highway.

There is no prize for guessing which regular visiting fisherman the hotel's Tatlow's Cellar bottle shop is named after. A now-blocked tunnel goes from the hotel, under Church Street, to former convict cells and the police station. Convicts building the hotel went to and from their toil in the tunnel so they could not scarper. The spire of the former Methodist (now Uniting) Church (1885) presides romantically on a rise among trees just south of the village.

Below by the river is an important historic site, part of Ross' grim convict women's work prison, called the Female Factory. Hundreds of women, a lot in their teens, were incarcerated there from 1847 to 1854. One of four main female factories in the colony, this is claimed to be the most archaeologically-intact one in the nation, but little remains above ground. The historic site is open to the public. The Overseer's Cottage's display includes a model of the place in 1851. Scores of the wretched convict women's nameless babes are buried nearby.

In the very early 1800s, Van Diemen's Land was stupidly divided into two counties, each with a governor. Cornwall was in the north and Buckinghamshire in the south. The separation line was the 42nd parallel of latitude, just north of Ross.

Ross district grazier, lawyer and former State Government Minister, John Bennett, blowing his trumpet, a souvenir from Page's colonial coaches. See silhouette No. 3. Photo, Tony Hope.

PART TEN 160 km
Campbell Town, Highland Lakes, Bothwell
Plus side trips to Arthurs Lake, Western Lakes, Waddamana

CAMPBELL TOWN, on the Elizabeth River 12 kms north of Ross, is another marvellous historic town that played an important part in the development of Tasmania. It, too, was named in 1821 by Australia's ubiquitous place namer, Governor Macquarie, when he camped here on his way to Hobart, this time, like streets and places elsewhere, after his wife. But it lived up to its name by attracting Scots Presbyterian settlers.

He renamed the village's Relief Creek the Elizabeth River, also after said wife, the former Elizabeth Campbell. The Aborigines called it the Parndokennerlyenpinder, roughly meaning river flowing from where the sun rises. The Governor then named the Macquarie River after himself. On his trip here 10 years earlier, the governor had named the district north of the village Macquarie Plains.

Two stage coaches thunder through what was then called Campbelltown in 1874.
Woodcut from the Illustrated Australian News.

These illustrations of slayings, titled Murders in Tasmania, *were published in the* Illustrated Australian News, *on 16 May 1883, during a trial of notorious Tasmanian murderers. They probably scared off potential new settlers.*

Macquarie made it an army garrison town. An enormous eucalypt tree trunk in the town's central park indicates the sort of forests that flourished around this important farming district. The Heritage Highway Museum and Visitor Information Centre in the main street has brochures marking history walks in the town.

The Fox Hunters Return, built by convicts from 1833 near the Red Bridge, Campbell Town.

The main street footpath features a long row of imbedded red bricks inscribed with the names and details about colonial convicts. Michael Tatlow officiated at the opening of the row, mostly paid for brick by brick by convicts' descendants. The fascinating memorial is a continuing project.

Old icons in **Campbell Town** are the 1841 Red Bridge, the oldest large bridge still on the highway, and the Fox Hunters Return by the bridge, now a superior boutique b. & b. It was built as a coaching inn by convicts with Irish stone mason Hugh Kean from 1833. The National Trust lists it as, "The finest and most substantial hotel building of the early colonial period in Australia". Foxes introduced for hunting were wiped out in the 1800's. But a few ship stowaways may now roam the state, threatening native animals. A task force is hunting them. A landmark building is the rambling replica of a Tudor gothic manor house behind the park. This is The Grange, designed by James Blackburn and built for Dr William Valentine in 1849. It was from here in a small observatory still standing that teacher Alfred Biggs and Valentine recorded the transit of Venus on 9 December 1874. Biggs also, less than two years after its invention by Alexander Graham Bell in USA in 1876, made the first long-distance telephone call in Tasmania to Launceston using the electric telegraph wires along the railway and with instruments he made himself. These are on display at the Queen Victoria Museum in Launceston.

As you leave Campbell Town, on the left is a memorial to local hero, the pioneer aviator Harold Gatty. This grandson of an Irish highwayman invented a ground speed and drift indicator, the basis for today's automatic pilot. Gatty accompanied American Wylie Post in their record-breaking flight around the world in eight days in 1931.

Turn westerly, off the highway, near the northern end of Campbell Town to join the sealed C522 Macquarie Road. This goes through early-settled sheep and cattle grazing land which, like other parts of the midlands, often suffers from drought. The early settlers expected this district to be as bountiful as the well-watered fields of England. It took them some years to adjust to the reality of dry farming with a short growing season. Our heritage therefore here is large holdings, sparse population and old villages that were expected to be large market towns but ceased growing a century and a half ago.

About 10 km from Campbell Town, turn left and cross the Macquarie River you last saw at Ross. Past the river, turn right at the nearby T-junction, still the C522, towards Cressy.

Importantly, some 20 kms along this interesting road, turn left on the B51 to Poatina, Aboriginal for a cavern. This is a touring adventure of a lifetime. Like ragged battlements of a mighty fort, the mountains of the Great Western Tiers leading to the Central

Tassie tourers taking a break about 1930. Colin Dennison Collection.

We suppose it was the wind.

Plateau rear before you. The road leaves the flat farmland to climb dramatically, zigging and zagging, to this former village settlement for hydro-electricity supply workers. The power station draws on massive Great Lake, a virtual inland sea, enlarged by dams, you will see soon. Cold highland water is piped down to Brumbys Creek

Harvest time by the road from Campbell Town to the Highlands.

The girls, having a spell.

at **Cressy**, another superb trout fishing location, to join the Macquarie. The views of the flattest part of Tasmania from lookouts on your way are spectacular. The Central Plateau you have mounted is like an inverted bowl, the sides of which rise abruptly from all points of the compass. The sunken centre-piece of the bowl holds Great Lake and uncounted thousands of other lakes, lagoons, tarns and streams, all hosting trout. Much of it is often clothed in snow in winter.

Wildlife is plentiful, notably in summer. Especially on a quiet evening or early morning, you may well see around here wallabies, wombats, platypuses, possums, quoll, wedge-tail eagles, raven-like currawongs, parrots, kookaburras, ducks of several varieties, black swans and even deer, which have thrived in small herds in the island's remote bushland since pioneer settlers introduced the animals' ancestors from Britain for hunting.

Arthurs Lake

IF YOU SEEK a camping site in light bushland on the margin of Tasmania's most popular trout fishery, turn left at a sign about 35km from Poatina to large Arthurs Lake, named after the island's most-remembered, perhaps most infamous, governor. It is a fine spot for a couple of days of relaxing but the weather at this altitude can quickly turn cold and windy.

The lake is the result of the then Hydro-Electric Commission flooding two lakes, leaving five islands. A pipeline from a pump house takes water to Great Lake, which drains to the power station at Poatina.

THE GRAND TOUR continues south on the B51 to its junction with the A5 Highland Lakes Road, where you turn left to leave the Lake Country for the largest expanse of hilly grazing country in the island on the way to old Bothwell, 45 km away.

As you slowly descend, you pass through cattle and sheep high country runs where livestock are still driven to summer pastures from grazing properties below. In the past, shepherding and droving provided an occupation for many. Relics of this period abound. The Wilson cottage at the Steppes (1863) is a preserved monument to this era. But first, consider a wondrous side trip:

Great Lake and the Western Lakes

TO TAKE THIS OPTION, if you have an extra day, turn right at the junction of the B51 and the A5, where you can rejoin the Grand Tour later. This takes you to the southern end of Great Lake through the mostly fishing-shack village of **Miena**, 14 km away. The name is Aboriginal for lake.

On the rise just before Shannon Lagoon are small stands of distinctive, finely-limbed trees called cider gums. This diseased-looking lot, with filigree limbs that are nearly naked, suffering from perhaps phytophthora or the interferences of man, is alarmingly the last stand of cider gums in the wild. Tasmanian Aborigines are said to have drunk a bitter, ciderish concoction from sap they tapped from the trees. The bridge over a former stream from the lake to Shannon Lagoon on your left is the scene of the former Shannon Rise which attracted trout fishers from around the world until the lake's level was raised by a second dam.

Sometimes wild deer graze in the grassland across the highway from the Central Highlands Lodge at Miena. A few kms further is the Great Lake Hotel with a nearby general store and petrol retailer. Huge log fires usually await travellers at the lodge and the hotel.

As the naked foreshores show, continued dry weather and the water demands of Hydro Tasmania have caused the level of today's no-so-Great Lake to drop some 15 metres below its "normal" level, denying the lake of its once-pretty, forested and grassy shorelines. Unless there is a dramatic change in the weather pattern, this sorry scene may well remain the new normal.

Only if the weather is gentle in this exposed alpine country, the highest point of the Tour, continue north on the A5 Highland Lakes Road by the lake's western shore for 10 kms and turn west at the Inland Fisheries Service centre at **Liawenee**, regularly recorded as the coldest spot in the State. The word is Aboriginal for cold, fresh water.

In April to June, when the fishing season is closed at most places, hundreds of thousands of Great Lake trout swim up the canal here, nose to tail, to spawn in gravelly shallows. It is a stirring sight. IFS officers net some female trout and strip them of their eggs. These are artificially fertilized with sperm from males. The eggs hatch at fish nurseries for ultimate liberation in waters around the State that need restocking. The young that hatch naturally eventually make their way back to the lake to grow. The majority that elude fishers and cormorants repeat the breeding cycle.

A drive west beside the canal feeding Great Lake on the quite-okay gravel road for about 20 minutes from Liawenee takes you to the starkly magnificent Western Lakes country. You will quickly see why this bleak, scrubby land of a thousand lakes above the winter snow-line, punctuated by rocky outcrops, has been the location for documentary films set in the days of the dinosaurs.

The largest lake is the first you see, Augusta. Drive across its dam and continue for a few kms and, if the weather is fair, walk among the alpine heath. One dip of a finger will tell you how cold the lake water is. The climate at this sacred fishery is as fickle as a highland trout so, unless you're a toughened bush walker, don't go out of sight of your vehicle.

Out for a Sunday drive on the horse railway near Waddamana in 1921. Colin Dennison Collection.

The hydro-electric Power Museum, Waddamana. Photo, Tony Hope.

DETOUR OPTION

To Waddamana

BACK ON THE GREAT LAKE side of the junction of the Highland Lakes Road and the B51 from Poatina, you have the option of turning right on the C177 gravel road nearly 1 km west of the junction. This takes you past the small trout fishing haven of Penstock Lagoon to visit the Hydro-electric Power Museum at the old hydro settlement of **Waddamana**. The Aboriginal word means big river. It is one of several locations to which Hydro Tasmania presented Aboriginal names. Work commenced on the Waddamana power station in 1911 as a private venture. Freezing conditions in the winter of 1912 made work in the mud and slush almost unbearable. Eventually a horse-drawn wooden tramway was built to take people, supplies and equipment. The company went broke and the government took over its completion. Its building attracted world-wide attention.

The first power was transmitted to Hobart in 1916. This encouraged the expansion of the city's electric tram system and the arrival of heavy industry in the State with construction of a zinc refinery and a carbide plant. The central highlands teemed with hydro-electric-power development workers in the 1950s and 60s, mostly European men who had fled the chaos after World War II. Waddamana Station was decommissioned when the Poatina station began operating in 1965.

Turn left a few kms south of Waddamana for an interesting 25 km drive on the C178 past **Hermitage** where the Shannon River sweeps south from Great Lake to join the River Derwent. Turn south back on the A5 and motor through former bushranger country, now mostly grazing land, to rejoin the Grand Tour.

THE LOVELY TOWN of **Bothwell** on the gentle Clyde River was settled mainly by Scots from 1824. Convicts despatched to the area included some Young Irelanders, imprisoned for "seditious utterances" about English occupation of Ireland.

Bothwell nestles in a broad valley surrounded by gently rolling farmland. The district was once a major producer of grains and fine wool. It was also popular with the Big River Aborigines, probably because of its abundant game.

It is named after Bothwell on the River Clyde in Scotland. A military barracks built in 1832 was named Fort Wentworth and later used as a convict watch house. It is on the western side of the Clyde River overlooking the town.

This is another early Tasmanian village that grew rapidly in the beginning and then stopped. It has much the same population as it had in the 1840s. Its many early colonial buildings and quiet setting with a village green justify a stroll around the town and perhaps a picnic beside the Clyde River on the Croakers Alley Historical Walk. Tulips add colour in October and roses through most of summer. Also see the unique four-sided sundial built as a World War I memorial in Queens Park. Those who like a wee dram of the doings should not miss the Nant Distillery and flour mill.

Bothwell is the home of the first Aberdeen Angus cattle stud in Australia and also has the oldest golf course in the southern hemisphere, founded by Scots pioneer Alexander Reid on his estate Ratho. The newly-upgraded course and splendid exhibition in the Australasian Golf Museum and information centre at Ratho are a mecca for golfers.

Generations were educated at the 1887 Bothwell School.

Bothwell's illustrious 1831 Coffee Palace, looking remarkably like the Fox Hunters Return at Campbell Town.

PART ELEVEN 100 km
Hamilton, Ouse, Tarraleah

A QUITE GOOD road (the B110) goes 30 km south from Bothwell through fine-wool sheep grazing country and bush land, past **Hollow Tree**, to the A10 Lyell Highway a few kms east of the also-ancient village of **Hamilton** on the River Clyde.

Georgian Hamilton was named Hamilton-on-Clyde by Governor Sorell in 1824 after a period dubbed Macquarie's Township after you-know-who. It has an interesting collection of colonial buildings of sandstone quarried and laid by convicts. In 1835 the population of the district included 309 convicts. 1840 saw the construction of the fine Glen Clyde House. The former coaching inn is now a Tasmanian craft gallery and cafe we recommend to the right as you

A dash of ancient Greece at Prospect Villa, Hamilton.

Glen Clyde House
Circa 1840 Hamilton Tasmania
A 'Must Stop' between Hobart and Strahan

- ⚘ Licensed Cafe
- ⚘ Tasmanian Craft Gallery
- ⚘ Information Centre
- ⚘ Alfresco Dining
- ⚘ Gardens
- ⚘ Takeaways

www.glenclyde.com

Lyell Highway Hamilton 7140
6286 3276

A load of sheep skins about 1900 at Hamilton's then Glen Clyde Hotel, now the meritorious Glen Clyde House restaurant. The cart driver looks to be in leg irons.

enter the town. It sells our favourite pies and has a wonderful European garden with a fountain out the back. By 1844 Hamilton was a farming centre with two breweries, at least six taverns, many sly-grog shops dispensing rum and beer at kitchen tables, wind and water mills, quarries and a convict probation station. Another gracious old oasis in the usually-dry hills around Hamilton is the Greco Italian renaissance-style garden behind 1840s Prospect Villa, which is open to the public. It is on Hamilton Plains Road just before the bridge over the Clyde.

The highway continues near meandering Lake Meadowbank, part of the River Derwent system, through fertile farming land and the oddly-named village of **Ouse**, by the River Ouse. This area became a major soldier resettlement dairy farm centre after World War II.

Local lore says the original name was Ooze, given the spot by pioneer coach drivers who were bogged in a sticky swamp they had to cross. Alas, not so. The name comes banally from Yorkshire's Ouse river basin, England.

Farming country ends soon after Ouse. 23 kms on is the former hydro-electricity village of **Wayatinah** (Aboriginal for a creek), where the highway crosses the River Nive after plunging down steep sub-alpine valleys. Wayatinah village is a couple of kms left from the highway beside pretty Wayatinah Lagoon, with plenty of smallish brown trout. Water from here spills south to turbines at a power station on the River Derwent.

The Lyell Highway's serious climb back to the Central Highlands to the rugged, wet and spectacular West Coast begins here. Dense patches of ferns and eucalyptus, blackwood, myrtle and sassafras trees are marred here and there by pine plantations to fuel the State's timber industries.

You are now back in hydro-electricity country. The highway levels for a while at a canal and massive pipes that you can drive beside into the reborn village of **Tarraleah**. This intriguing little alpine resort is regularly clothed in snow in winter. So, incidentally, having the likes of orange balls is essential if you fancy a game of golf here amongst snowdrifts. But the locals can supply luminous balls for night golf!

Tarraleah was an Aboriginal name for a kangaroo and you are likely to see plenty of wallabies and possums around here at sunset and dawn. Your authors often see wedge-tail eagles and black cockatoos here, too, among Tarraleah's 80 resident bird species. The black, raven-like birds with white emblazoned tails that you see plenty of are currawongs, often called black jays. They are highland residents replacing Tasmania's cunning lowland scavenger ravens, commonly and wrongly called crows. Currawongs are smart characters, not much scared of humans and bold thieves at a picnic.

A path over the penstocks near the restaurant leads to an enchanting, easy walk in the wil-

Boys of the bush brigade in the late 1900s. They often took on raging forest fires.

Now gone, the amazing Butlers Gorge village for dam construction workers about 1950. Black & White Photographics.

Payday for hydro power construction workers in 1948. Next stop, the pub?

Stuck in the snow, about 1950. Times were tough in winter for power workers and their families in the Highlands.

Penstocks plunge water from Tarraleah to drive turbines at the power station in the Nive River valley.

derness, overlooking waterfalls, for an hour or so. The view from The Lodge and the restaurant across the Nive River valley and the Tarraleah and Tungatinah power stations is awesome.

Tarraleah was built for power station workers from 1934 to 1938. Tasmania operates 29 power stations with an installed capacity of 2,570 megawatts. Cables take some of the electricity under Bass Strait to Victoria, which in turn sells electricity back to Tasmania when the hydro supply runs short.

The 5-star art-deco Lodge is the former digs for Hydro-Electric Commission bosses. Former workers' cottages nearby have been upgraded for family holiday accommodation.

A wedge-tail eagle, our biggest but now also a rare bird you are likely to see around Tarraleah. Colin Dennison Collection.

Many flocks of raucous smart and timid black cockatoos live in the highlands but favour the lowlands in bleak weather. Photo, Geoff Love.

SNAPSHOT 1952

The Devil ate the minister

LITTLE CHARLIE WOOLEY sat fidgeting beside his mother Ella with the congregation in the church in the raw settlement of Tarraleah one bleak Sunday morning in 1952, waiting for their Anglican minister to arrive.

The Wooleys had migrated from the Isle of Arran, on the Scottish side of the Irish Sea, a couple of years before, when Charlie was two. His late father, also Charles, was a power station operator. It had been a remote and rugged introduction to the antipodes.

Worshippers gradually left the church, deciding that the minister must have become lost on his regular pre-church walk in the forest. Charlie and mum walked home to their cottage, fearful like the rest of the village for their pastor out there in the wilds.

Organised searches failed to find him. One day young Charlie heard a couple of local bushmen talking about it. "We'll never find his body, you know," one said. "Maybe only his clothes. The devils'll eat him, for sure."

"Scary stuff, it was, for a little kid who thought the devil lived in hell to hear that there was more than one of them and they lurked out there in the bush," Charlie recalls. "Sometimes after that when I heard devils screaming in the night I'd hide my head under the blankets.

"Tarraleah, though, had a sort of wild magic about it that probably implanted my love of, my passion to preserve, this amazing island's natural environment."

No remains of the minister were ever found. Tasmanian devils still live around here, but the numbers of these nocturnal marsupials about the size of a spaniel have been sorely reduced in many areas recently by an infectious and fatal facial tumour disease. The devils were named by pioneer settlers who were spooked by the growling and shrieking at night from these black meat eaters. In fact, devils are gregarious critters whose scary cries are mostly bluff. We believe they have never attacked a human. Not a live one, anyway.

A Highlands log train, c. 1925.

Plugger Wooley addressing a leak in an old hydro-electricity pipeline.

PART TWELVE 80 km
Bronte Lagoon, Lake St Clair

THIS IS THE shortest section of the Grand Tour, but there is so much natural beauty to enjoy! If you are not counting the days, it might also be the longest.

Take care in winter travelling from Tarraleah to Queenstown, where the Lyell Highway can become crusted with ice and snow. The highway curls and plunges abruptly from Tarraleah village through ferned forest to the Nive River and the Tarraleah and Tungatinah power stations.

The road then climbs steeply to the Central Plateau beside a chain of three lakes 650 metres above sea level and connected by canals. They were formed by damming and channeling for years from 1950, flooding ancient marshes. The first is Tungatinah Lagoon, from where penstocks plunge water to feed the Tungatinah power station.

Then come Lake Binney and deep Bradys Lake. Several tracks off the highway go to popular fishing and camping locations. To get a closer look at these impressive impoundments, turn right off the highway and go along the top of Binney Dam on the lake's northern shore. This fair gravel road continues north beside majestic Bradys Lake's western shore, bordered by scores of holiday shacks. Tasmanians call even a lavish bushland holiday home a shack.

Trout and released giant Atlantic salmon populate these lakes, the names of which your authors think encapsulate the egalitarianism of Tasmanians. Tungatinah is, of course, an Aboriginal word. It means a shower of rain. Lake Binney is named after the State's most elite, a Tasmanian governor. And the biggest, Bradys Lake, immortalises notorious escaped convict bushranger Matthew Brady.

The lakeside road rejoins the Lyell Highway less than a kilometre south of a bridge over The Whitewater which surges from Bronte Lagoon, depending on the needs of Hydro Tasmania and sometimes white-water kayakers.

You will get glimpses of beautiful Bronte Lagoon through the trees on your left. Stop for a while at the reserve just before the bridge over the canal that flows into the lagoon. A monument here, the geographical centre of Tasmania, commemorates the early surveyors who explored and mapped it.

A five-minute diversion on the bitumen road a little further along on the right will get you to the settlement of **Bronte Park**, where there is a chalet, camping and cottage accommodation, and a general store that sells petrol.

Back heading west, the Lyell Highway goes through rolling, in places wild, country; the scene of early sheep grazing in summer. This is particularly noticeable where you cross the picturesque Nive River. Assistant Surveyor William Sharland, the first white man to explore this land in 1832, recommended the tussock plains as good grazing land. Lots were offered cheaply but harsh winters soon convinced would-be settlers that this bleak land was for only summer pasturing. A township site called Marlborough was surveyed in the 1840s at the Nive crossing and a police station was established. As you can see, it was a town that never was. Further on is a remarkable

Greg Duncan with part of his amazing creation of carved wood murals at The Wall in the Wilderness, near Derwent Bridge. Photo, James Lauritz.

The marker in front of the bushes honours pioneer surveyors at this absolute centre of Tasmania beside Bronte Lagoon, a favourite troutery for a couple of your authors.

attraction, The Wall in the Wilderness. It has a brilliant display of Greg Duncan's honey-coloured Huon pine carved murals and figures, many of them depicting Tasmanian history. When completed, the history mural will be 100 metres long.

A couple of kms on is the village of **Derwent Bridge**, named for its little bridge over the headwater that grows and flows south to become the mighty River Derwent at Hobart. Your authors regularly brace the bar, dine and stay at the Derwent Bridge Wilderness Hotel. The bar, lounge and dining room are in a cathedral-like room of vaulted native timbers, divided by two whopping great fireplaces.

Leeawulenna, the sleeping water, is the apt and romantic name Aborigines had for the enchanting lake you really should explore by taking the bitumen road north for about 10 minutes through bushland from beside the bridge. Members of the Big River tribe moved

A high-country beach, Lake St Clair.

here and built huts of bark thousands of years ago as glaciers from the last ice age retreated. The huts and charcoal drawings on their wall were destroyed by red-neck white bushmen.

This is **Lake St Clair**. With an arrogance that rivalled place-name champion Governor Macquarie, surveyor General George Frankland named it this in 1835 to flatter a family of Scots, the St Clairs, in the colony where Aboriginal monikers were largely ignored. Surveyor William Sharland more culpably had named the impoundment Lake Gordon a few years earlier.

Right on the doorstep of some of Tasmania's best National Parks

DERWENT
BRIDGE
WILDERNESS
HOTEL

David & Carol Fitzgibbon
Proprietors

Lyell Hwy, Derwent Bridge
Phone (03) 6289 1144
fax (03) 6289 1173
Mobile 0408 104 113
dewentbridgewildernesshotel@bigpond.com

Rock hoppers at Lake St Clair.

The lake is an immense natural impoundment of deep, clear and usually sparkling water, home to a million trout, set among alpine peaks clothed in snow for much of the year. It even has little beaches of white sand near the visitor hospitality and information complex.

The Hydro Electricity Commission built a weir across the lake's southern outflow in 1937 to raise the water level 2.4 metres. Take a stroll, see some wildlife beside pristine Leeawulenna, lorded over from the west by the bulky, often cream-coated cake, Mount Olympus. At dawn or dusk it can be breathtaking.

Hobart lawyer and naturalist Morton Allport took this probably first wilderness photograph of Tasmania in 1863 when he took seven friends to Lake St Clair. They also climbed Mt Arrowsmith, with Allport's wife Lizzie still startling the natives in her ghostly crinolines. The Allport Library and Museum of Fine Arts in Hobart honours Morton's generous family. Allport Collection, State Library of Tasmania.

Photo, Charles Wooley

A theatre of awe

In the highland hush when the air is still
The lakes look polished beyond man's skill.
In mountain shade or orange demise
Of the sun on its wane
A trout will rise,
Rippling the sheen of the watery pane
In a humbling theatre of awe.　　　M.T.

Photo, Geoff Love

PART THIRTEEN 160 km
Queenstown, Strahan

Wattles add blazes of gold by the Lyell Highway nearing the West Coast.

THE DRIVE WEST of Derwent Bridge to Queenstown is a gob smacker. It goes at first through lightly-forested hills and button grass plains with mountains left and right. Pink, white and yellow wildflowers, including little orchids, glorify the pageant.

A lookout and monument by the road 10 km from Derwent Bridge recognises the hardy engineers and workers who built this extraordinary road from 1926 to 1932. From here we plunge to the West Coast; a different world. The firmament changes abruptly from eucalypt and grassy plains to dark, rain forests of blackwood, myrtle, sassafras, impenetrable horizontal scrub and flowering leatherwood trees that provide the State's unique honey. The white boxes stacked near the road in spring and summer are bee-keepers' hives.

Mosses and tree ferns are common here. In spring the acacias (wattles) bloom with splashes of gold. Eight kms of spectacular down-hill, winding road take you through Surprise Valley, its bordering peaks often endowed by an eerie mist.

Stop for a while at the Parks and Wildlife Service picnic area, with covered barbeque facilities, just before the bridge over the Franklin River. You can stroll in the forest on crushed white quartz paths in this wonderworld, assailed by the fragrant tang of the wilds, exhilarated by rushes of oxygen. The word wilderness is widely and misleadingly exploited in promotional material about this part of the world. You can, however, get a taste of true wilderness off the track in this forest. About 500 rafters leave from here every year on the, at times perilous, ride down the Franklin to the Gordon River.

Is it raining? If not, it probably will soon. Some places on the West Coast get three metres of rain a year. Moisture sucked from the Southern Ocean is driven by the Roaring Forties trade winds charging from South America, south of South Africa to Tasmania. The mountains here confront the rainclouds like fortresses to be stormed. So, over the coming days of the Tour, expect precipitation.

Your next place of wonderment is man-made Lake Burbury, a hydro-electricity catchment drowning the former King River valley and the old copper-smelting town of Crotty. It is deep and brooding, skirted by rugged mountain peaks which are often attired by snow in winter. We rate this and the natural Lake St Clair the grandest of all the lakes on the island. It is home to some big trout, too! The

Lake Burbury, deep in its glacial vale skirted by mountains and home to a lot of trout.

lake was named after our first Tasmanian-born governor, Sir Stanley Burbury. Many other hydro lakes are named after governors. You can drive to a sign-posted boat ramp and an extensive camping ground with toilets and covered cooking facilities just before the bridge that spans the impoundment. Ahead are 21 remarkable kms to Queenstown.

The highway passes geological mega structures such as folds in the 600-million-year-old rocks with large outcrops stained yellow and brown by iron. They are reminders of the vibrant days at the Mt Lyell copper and gold mine, where a tough breed of prospectors discovered valuable minerals aplenty in 1883.

At the head of the valley approaching Mount Lyell was the once bustling town of **Linda**, for a short time the headquarters of the North Lyell Mine, which had its own railway, smelters and even a port at Kelly Basin, at the south-east end of Port Macquarie. All that is left of Linda are the ruins of a hotel and a couple of cottages.

The Iron Blow open-cut mine in the mid 1900s, still making a mighty impression near Gormanston. Colin Dennison Collection.

Boot repairs and close shaves were on offer at this interesting establishment in the 1890s.

The cast of the film Jewelled Nights shot on the osmiridium fields at the West Coast's Savage River in the 1920s. The star was Louise Lovely, who ended up running a lolly shop in Hobart. Colin Dennison Collection.

The road climbs to, at your right, the famous Iron Blow. Specks of gold in a massive outcrop of ore here once glittered under the sun. A sample from the Iron Blow assayed at a bountiful 15 ounces of gold to the ton. A five-minute drive from the signpost on the right will give you a memorable view of it all. Nearby, back on the highway, some cottages remain of the lively mining town of **Gormanston**. This once had its own municipal council and a divided main street lined by shops and public buildings. West Coasters call it Gormie.

We know people who are too scared to travel on the steep, winding six kms of the highway down to **Queenstown**, through hills stripped of vegetation to fuel smelters. The processing change to pyritic smelting, the toxic sulphur fumes and heavy rain did the rest. The result is amazing; a showcase of what rampant mining did. Only lately, vegetation is slowly growing back.

"Queenie" was Tasmania's wild-west frontier town. Its miners and timber getters were hard working, hard drinking and hard playing men who played (and still play) Aussie Rules football on a ground of gravel. Old timers swear that, after the football, ravens and even gulls enticed from the coast scavenged in the gravel for morsels of flesh.

There were 14 pubs and cheap locally-made whisky galore. Gambling and brawling were rife. It still has the flavour of a frontier town but is now a more sober place, fascinating to stroll about in. Once the island's third largest town with 6,000 residents, fewer than half that number live here now. It is a friendly community, quick to support as one any family hit by tragedy. Such bonding grew, we suspect, from its isolation and disasters in the mines. 42 men were killed in an underground mine fire in 1912.

Queenstown was founded in 1896, about 30 years after the first fossickers were around, when today's near moonscape was dense rain-forest. British patriotism perhaps brought about its name (a change from Penghana) plus the Empire and Imperial hotels and the Queen River. Surveyor Philip Gidley King, however, named the King River, either after himself or his father, one-time Gover-

Laying the amazing Abt rail line about 1896, linking Queenstown and Strahan. It is now the West Coast Wilderness Railway.

Queenie boasts one of Australia's grandest post offices.

nor of NSW. The only communications with the rest of the world were by pack-horse east for weeks over the mountains to Hobart or on a rough track west to Strahan and its wharf. The coming of the Queenstown to Strahan Abt railway, a wonder of inventive engineering in 1896, replaced horses to lug ore and equipment to and from the wharf. The railway link with Burnie on the North-West Coast in the early 1900s further opened up the West Coast.

The opening in 1932 of the Lyell Highway to the delights of Hobart must have been like Queenie getting the keys to paradise. The Abt railway has been restored and renamed the West Coast Wilderness Railway, taking tourists from Queenstown and Strahan on alternating days on half-day trips through the rugged wilds. Steam locos use the rack and pinion Abt system under the loco and in the centre of the line to haul the trains up and ease them down steep parts of the route.

Call at the Galley Museum and visitor information centre in the former Imperial Hotel in Driffield Street for local guidance and to see an absorbing collection of early photographs and memorabilia.

In 1976, a geological survey discovered Aboriginal artifacts made from pink quartzite under the forest soil at 30 sites north and south-east of Queenstown. This discovery "suggests extensive inland habitation by the Aborigines prior to the establishment of the now-widespread rainforest".

In summer, communities of reddish wild orchids line parts of the 37-km road west through undulating bushland to **Strahan**. The top Tasmanian resort town by Macquarie Harbour is rich in boisterous, bloody history. It borders the highest-rating World Heritage rainforest on earth. The picturesque port, named after a governor of Tasmania in the 1880s, was once the British Empire's most remote outpost. Strahan was founded in 1880 and earlier known as Long Bay. It is the sole non-mining settlement on the West Coast, founded by pioneer merchant Frederick Ormiston Henry.

Dawn greeting the captivating cruise and fishing port of Strahan.

The first thing you should do here is visit the West Coast Visitor Information and Booking Centre at the wharf to find out more about the history of the region and the many water, air and wilderness tours and other activities available. The Strahan Village motel is just north of the wharf and, in a colonial garden near the foreshore around Strahan Point, is elegantly-restored Ormiston House, built for F. O. Henry in 1905. Ormiston's attic even has a museum.

The wharf is home to a busy fishing fleet and a mill processing the district's famous, now precious, Huon pine. The trees are unique to this region and the oldest living Tasmanians. They can live for more than 3,000 years, producing fine-grained timber the colour of honey, rich in oil and prized for making furniture and boats. After generations of heavy harvesting, the remaining trees are now protected. Only dead timber salvaged from the river banks is now milled.

Hells Gates is the treacherously-narrow channel linking the harbour with the Southern Ocean. Tidal currents have dashed scores of craft onto rocks the channel charges by. Michael Tatlow surfed through it from the ocean one hairy night in a little wooden fishing boat during a storm.

Swashbuckling young Captain James Kelly and his crew of four in a whale-boat were the first Europeans to run Hells

A cruise catamaran on the magical Gordon River. Courtesy Pure Tasmania, Federal Group.

And a rack-and-pinion loco on the line this year letting off steam while its lucky passengers dine at a station café and take a walk on the wild side.

Gates when circumnavigating the island colony in 1815. He craftily named Macquarie Harbour after his vain Governor in Sydney. And Kelly named the main river flowing into the harbour to immortalise James Gordon, who supplied the whale-boat. The mariner formed friendships with Aborigines living around the harbour, the Toogee tribe. Their women

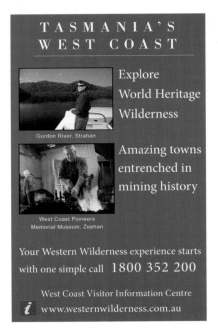

demonstrated to the whites how, smeared with seal fat, they joined groups of basking seals, snorting like the animals, before clubbing a few for food. Seals are smarter nowadays.

Kelly had named Port Davey to the south after Van Diemen's Land's then governor. We suspect the adventurer was rewarded for his harbour naming when he was appointed Harbour Master of Hobart Town.

The perceived worst of the worst of the colony's convicts, 1,200 men and women, were imprisoned from 1822 to 1833 on the harbour's pretty Sarah Island. Cruise tours take tourists daily to explore among the ruins of buildings on this six-hectare isle of the damned, the scene of so much depravity. In the late 1820s it was Australia's most productive ship-building yard. This included felling Huon pines and rafting logs down the freezing and sometimes rapid Gordon River. Some logs were two metres wide and 20 metres long. Many convicts were crushed to death.

West Coast Mayor Darryl Gerrity, the grandson of a driver on the Abt railway, tells the story of the Sarah Island superintendent who dispatched to the governor in Hobart Town three pages of bitter complaint about the island's doctor's mongrel dog molesting his pedigree bitch. The super's last line immodestly added, by the way: *7,000 lashes administered yesterday.* The governor mollified his military officer by giving him permission to have a whale killed and sell the meat. And also to "acquire" an Aboriginal girl "companion" while the dogs carried on outside. This for the master of this hellish

Ruins on Sarah Island.

A prized log of Huon pine being milled at Strahan's wharf.

A cruise catamaran passing through Hells Gates, the dangerous entrance from the Great Southern Ocean to Port Macquarie and once hellish times for convicts. Courtesy Pure Tasmania, Federal Group.

place in Eden, the keeper of hundreds of convicts driven to desperate misconduct in other institutions after being transported across the world for, mostly, petty thievery. There were also villains, brutalised by their treatment.

Perhaps the most notorious convict on the island was Irishman Alexander Pearce, transported for stealing six pairs of shoes. He escaped with seven others and amazingly made it, alone, to become a bushranger near Hobart. When caught, little Pearce said he had survived the trek by eating his companions. He preferred fresh human flesh, he said, over salted mutton. With no witnesses, a scoffing, unbelieving judge sent Pearce back to Sarah Island. He escaped again, with one other, and was caught alone with human limbs in a bag. Pearce the cannibal was hanged in Hobart in 1824.

In the 1980s Strahan was the hub of a bitter national argument

for and against a plan to dam the Gordon River, turning some of the lower Franklin River into a lake to generate hydro electricity. The pro-dam State Premier of the day called the Franklin River "a leech-ridden ditch". Federal intervention halted the project in 1984.

A local yarn says King George IV is buried in a small cave by the north-eastern shore of Macquarie Harbour. The cave has *King George IV*, carved long ago, above its entrance. We have checked it. No body. Never. The inscriber, we suppose, was a colonial joker.

The death mask of convict Alexander Pearce.

PART FOURTEEN 135 km
Zeehan, Rosebery, Cradle Mountain

Main street in the rip roaring mining town of Zeehan in 1891. West Coast Pioneers Memorial Museum.

DRIVE NORTH from Strahan on Andrew Street, which becomes Henty Road (the B27) for a 46 km trip to Zeehan on a fine road by old sand dunes, scrubby hills, many streams and vast pine plantations. The Zeehan-Strahan railway (1892 to the 1960s) which went this way was an important part of a 359-km network of rail and tramways through some of the toughest terrain in the world. Some of them had rails of wood.

You can divert for a while just out of Strahan, though, on the C250 to see magnificent and pristine Ocean Beach. The Hells Gates lighthouse is to the left and, north to your right, is 40 kms of beach usually pounded by foaming combers generated thousands of kms away in the Southern Ocean. It is Tasmania's longest beach. Mutton birds (short-tailed shearwaters) nest in the sand dunes. A timber lookout platform beside the B27 as it climbs away from dune and button grass country gives a grandstand view of the coast.

Zeehan is named after one of explorer Abel Tasman's ships. It was the "silver city"; a rip-roaring, booming mining town in the late 1800s and the first couple of decades of the 1900s. For a short time it hosted Australia's busiest stock exchange. In 1891, 79 mining companies operated around here. Assays showed an average 76 per cent lead and 70 ounces of silver to the ton. Zinc was also plentiful, but unwanted. A population that reached 8,000 has fallen to fewer than 800. But Zeehan still has the trappings of its glory days, with hopes of renewal.

The ground under and around the town is a catacomb of disused mining tunnels, some only a little below the surface. Many a modern fossicker has fallen into them. One tunnel, from the former Spray mine tramway, is big enough to drive through. Apparent muddy little potholes can be old mine shafts. So do not go rambling around Zeehan.

The town's major attraction is the West Coast Pioneers Memorial Museum in the main street with its collection of old West Coast locos on the corner. Originally the Zeehan School of Mines, it has a world-class collection of minerals, crystals and gemstones from every corner of the earth. Also mining machinery and memorabilia and hundreds of photographs of old mining operations, road and rail travel, long-gone mining towns and rugged looking bush pioneers.

A splendid and funny private folk museum is at the home of resident character and former miner Ray (Shorty) Keating in Shaw Street, four streets north on the right from the Pioneer's Museum.

Zeehan's 'Shorty' Keating at his amazing home museum, complete with a little mine, in Shaw Street.

Shorty welcomes visitors. You will know the place from the display, including a replica bush hut, in front. Shorty has rooms full of mineral specimens, fossils, timber-getting and convict gear, and a skip of ore in a recreated mine tunnel.

The grand old Gaiety Theatre in the town centre can seat 1,000. Miners loaded

"The Opera House". The Gaiety, the pride of Zeehan, hosted performances by Enrico Caruso and Harry Houdini, but not Dame Nellie Melba. Part of the theatre was once the posh Grand Hotel.

with money attracted world entertainment celebrities to the Gaiety. Performers included American escapologist Harry Houdini, Italian tenor Enrico Caruso and in 1924, nearly everyone around bragged to us, our world famous songbird Dame Nellie Melba.

We asked at the Pioneer's Museum to see photographs of Dame Nellie's big night in town. None was available, though. How odd, your diligent authors thought. We snooped about. Official websites, published articles and locals in a pub told us about the soprano's dazzling performance. A Pioneers Museum staffer, pressed again, said Nellie was definitely booked to perform at the Gaiety, which some locals call the Opera House. "But, no," she admitted. "There's no written record of her show."

A traitorous local eventually whispered the awful truth. And a Zeehan history buff confirmed when challenged that the story of Dame Nellie Melba packing out the Gaiety is an astonishing hoax that, until this book, has fooled even Zeehan residents.

Nellie loved a drop of the doings. After a concert in Burnie, she got drunk. Hung over next morning, the diva dame was in no condition to make the train trip to a gutted Zeehan. West Coast Mayor, Darryl Gerrity, laughingly confirmed this. "It's high time the old hoax was exposed," he told us.

Dame Nellie Melba, who once took a bath in the pourings from 152 bottles of Champagne.

Captivating motoring of 108 kms to Cradle Mountain is ahead through raw, thriving rainforest in valleys between bleak peaks and over streams. In places the thick scrub and trees arch over the road making it seem like a tunnel. Drive 5 km east on the B27 road from Zeehan to Queenstown, then turn left on the Zeehan Highway (the A10) to wind north through the silver, lead and zinc mining settlement of **Rosebery**, 24 km away. For many years its only link with the outside was by rail. It wasn't until the late 1950s that Rosebery got a road to Queenstown, then to Burnie in the 1960s.

Timber getting the hard way, before today's clear-fellers. These men were at the confluence of the Nora and Bird Rivers, West Coast, in 1900. West Coast Pioneers Memorial Museum.

Fossickers for precious osmiridium in the early 1900s. The metal sold for a thousand pounds an ounce. West Coast Pioneers Memorial Museum.

Superb engineering and a lot of sweat constructed the Dundas tramway, from Zeehan to Williamsford. Here, a Sharpe & Stewart G class loco is lugging passenger carriages past the Montezuma Falls in 1899. Colin Dennison Collection.

Rosebery boasts of having the last postcode in the nation: 7470. It also gets pretty wet, with an astonishing 3.5 metres of rain a year. Prospector Tom McDonald found gold around here in 1893. The town's name was given three years later and it has nothing to do with flowers or fruit. It comes from the Prime Minister of England at the time, Lord Rosebery.

The next stop, on what is now the Murchison Highway, is over rain-forested Mt Murchison to the former silver-lead mining village of **Tullah.** For many years it was the most isolated community in Tasmania. Its only link with the outside world was a narrow-gauge tramway to the Emu Bay Railway line north to Burnie. Part of the track, some rolling stock and a little locomotive named Wee Georgie Wood after a famous British comedian of the time, are now working tourist attractions. Little remains of the original town, on a rise above long, magnificent and winding Lake Rosebery, formed by the Bastyan Dam. This was named after yet another governor!

Miners' family picnic day at Muddy Creek, late 1800s. The women and children travelled in one carriage, the men in others. Colin Dennison Collection.

Modern Tullah is the survivor of a once-large Hydro-Electric construction village. Many of the village's small homes here were carted on trucks from closing-down hydro-electricity villages on the West Coast. Turn left past the surprisingly big shopping centre to the fine Lakeside Chalet accommodation centre and restaurant amid trees beside, of course, the lake.

The Tullah Tavern boasts the record of 41, the most 18-gallon barrels of beer drunk at one establishment in all of Australia in a week during the town's Hydro boom years in the 1980s, when the population was 2,500 compared with today's 200. The tavern is now a café and museum.

The enchanting Lakeside Chalet at Tullah.

28 km on, turn right off the A10 and follow the signs for 38 kms of alpine country through forests and open button-grass plains to **Cradle Mountain.** Early Van Diemen's Land Company explorer Henry Hellyer likened this country to a nobleman's domain and named the Surrey Hills and Middlesex Plains. They were initially used for sheep pasturing, with disastrous results. More about that later.

Take one look at the twin peaks behind the unforgettable resort and you will see why Cradle Mountain was named so. Another VDL Company explorer, Joseph Fossey, dubbed it in 1828, a change from Ribbed Rock. At 1,545 metres above sea level, it is the fifth highest of the countless peaks on the island. Many of our mere hills, you might now realise, would be called mountains in most other places.

Summer kayakers on glorious Dove Lake in front of Cradle Mountain. Courtesy Pure Tasmania, Federal Group.

The view of the mountain from across Dove Lake, the peaks inverted in a mirror in summer and awesomely bleak and snowy in winter, is probably the most photographed scene in Tasmania. Try to see it, too, at sunset. The sky at remote Tasmanian centres like this on a clear night, free of air pollution and electric lights, is a sparkling spectacle with the Milky Way looking close enough to touch.

You can get directions from the Parks and Wildlife Service centre, from where walkers begin the one-way 65-km Overland Track trek south to Lake St Clair. Recreations include night animal tours, canoeing on Lake Dove, fishing and scenic flights. The Cradle Mountain Lodge complex has a big Wilderness Gallery Interpretation Centre.

Like so many people from other countries who came to this island, fell in love with it, stayed and set examples in appreciation and preservation of its environment, Austrians Gustav and Kate Weindorfer trekked through the bush and built a wood cabin near Cradle Mountain in 1912. Their home Waldheim (forest home) is now a chalet and gallery amid myrtles, King Billy pines and pandani, a giant grass tree endemic to Tasmania.

PART FIFTEEN 165 km
Waratah, Wynyard, Stanley
Tales of King Island, side trip to Rocky Cape

Magnificent Waratah, rich in mining heritage and built by a waterfall.

BACK AT THE Cradle Mountain turnoff at the A10 Murchison Highway, motor north for 16 km and turn left on the B23 for about five kms to visit eye-popping **Waratah**.

The now-spick village of 300 residents with a deep waterfall in its midst is the birthplace of mining in Tasmania. Over this waterfall a once-fabulous tin mine's crushing plant and dressing sheds were powered by a large waterwheel. The first hydro-electric power plant in Australia was set up in 1883, initially to light the works at night.

Revered pioneer James "Philosopher" Smith discovered the nearby Mount Bischoff tin deposit in 1871. Mining began a couple of years later in terrible conditions as the mount was covered by one of the densest jungles on earth. It was mightily rich, shedding rocks of pure tin at times but isolated until connected to Burnie by rail.

The camp at Mt Bischoff, the "Mountain of Tin" near Waratah in 1878. Woodcut from the Illustrated Australian News.

Philosopher Smith, discoverer of Waratah's tin. Also iron, lead and silver at Penguin.

In the 1880s and 1890s, bustling Waratah's population soared to about 3,000. Mount Bischoff was rated the richest tin mine in the world. It put Burnie on the path to becoming a major port and gave untold riches to some lucky families in Launceston.

A replica of Philosopher Smith's hut is beside the old courthouse, now the Waratah Museum which is packed with memorabilia and old photographs. A walking track goes several kms south-west to an old powerhouse and a ghost town by the former Magnet silver mine. Nix Creek around here, incidentally, was named by a prospector who found the stream unproductive. We assume they had more luck in the town's Happy Valley.

After Waratah, the Murchison Highway goes north through the Hellyer Gorge State Reserve. It is the last rain forest you will see on our Tour, unless you later visit the far north-west's Tarkine.

Big tree plantations are on the way north to undulating farmland at **Henrietta** and **Yolla**. This is rich dairy and beef cattle country with productive crops of vegetables and opium poppies for the world's pharmaceuticals industry. Early mornings and on late afternoons you might be pleasantly stopped on the road, as we were, by herds of cows with inflated udders crossing from their paddocks to milking sheds.

Yolla is an Aboriginal name for mutton-bird. Be careful that you take the left fork here onto Mount Hicks Road, the B26, down to the North West Coast just east of **Wynyard**. Continue straight ahead, around the traffic roundabout on the Bass Highway that bypasses Wynyard, remaining on Mount Hicks Road to the coast. Go left beside the shore on the *Old* Bass Highway into this marvellous centre of 4,500 residents astride the Inglis River.

Wynyard is a pretty, largely dormitory town for Burnie that also supports the district's farms. Many retirees live here, too, so take care walking in the shopping centre in Goldie Street so you are not skittled by a motorised wheelchair.

Navigator Matthew Flinders, who charted so much of Australia, named the sometimes turbulent sea before you Bass's Strait in 1798 after his shipmate, surgeon George Bass, in the voyage that proved that Van Diemen's Land was an island.

John King liked the look of the place from the sea in 1841 and cleared forest for a house and farm at the site of the Wynyard Golf Course across the Inglis River. His nearest neighbours were at Stanley for four years until King drowned in the Cam River. Some years later, men splitting eucalypt wood for roofing in Victoria or the Lands Department named the settlement after the commander of British troops in the Australian Colonies, General Edward Wynyard.

Cows heading for the milking shed rightly have right of way at Yolla.

Wynyard's Camp Creek bridge and Stutterd's store and residence c. 1900. Stutterd's was the town's first shop. Photo courtesy, Lyn Connellan, White Dog Book Cafe, which was Stutterd's No. 2 store.

Timber splitting led to Manxmen Robert Quiggin and William Moore establishing a large sawmilling operation in 1853. Moore later entered the Tasmanian Parliament and prospered enough to retire to Tynwald at New Norfolk. (See page 130). Tynwald is the name of the parliament on Britain's Isle of Man, whose residents are Manxmen. From the sawmilling period the town grew steadily, with red-letter days such as when Tasmania's first butter factory opened there in 1892, the railway came from the east in 1913 and the airport opened in 1936.

The Visitor Information Centre has a Wonders of Wynyard exhibition that features Francis Ransley's collection of early Ford vehicles including the equally-oldest Ford car in the world.

The Table Cape district is a major attraction for visitors and the magnificent scenic route along the towering sea cliffs is evocative of the coastline of Devon and Cornwall in England. Fewer than 150 years ago, huge forests covered this sublime farmland; its red and chocolate soils patch-worked with fields of blooming tulips in spring, sheep and cattle thriving on green grasses most of the year, potatoes, baled hay late in summer and pyrethrum to make insecticide. We assume here are no flies on Table Cape when the pyrethrum flowers.

The volcanic core of Table Cape looms over the Strait. Its guiding light was built in 1888. Signposted Murdering Gully Road here is the scene of an 1850 ugly murder that has not been solved.

Victim Samuel Oakes' body was partly burned. Visitors are welcome to explore at Fossil Bluff, north of the mouth of the Inglis. It is rich in fossils of animals, shells and vegetation. A few hundred metres west along the coast are neat rows of stones partly blocking off a natural inlet. These and other such structures along the coast were traps for fish that swam on incoming tides through a gap left in the rocks. At high tide the gap was filled with more rocks, or perhaps the trap makers themselves, leaving the fish high and dry and ready to be picked up at low tide.

Many think the traps are the ancient work of Aborigines. Not so. The North-West's fish traps were made by colonials. Examination of middens at Rocky Cape west of here indicated that Aborigines stopped eating scale fish 10,000 years ago. Perhaps a group died from eating fish with poisonous flesh such as toad-fish and the word got around. The town has a popular aero club. REX airline has many flights a day between Wynyard and Melbourne.

To the Cape's Murdering Gully, scene of an unsolved and grizzly slaying.

The lighthouse at Table Cape, a volcanic plug and patchwork of lush crops including tulips.

The thin line of rocks, mid picture left, at Wynyard were laid by pioneer whites at Wynyard just east of Table Cape to trap fish.

THE KING ISLAND FARCE

TAS AIR flies nearly half way across the Strait to Tasmania's **King Island** from Wynyard, also from Devonport and Hobart.

The island was the scene of a farcical performance by the British Navy in December 1802. French explorer Nicolas Baudin's scientific expeditioners were temporarily camped on King Island when a British Navy ship sailed up. It had been despatched by Sydney's Governor King, who wrongly reckoned the French were land-grabbers like him. The Brits took a longboat ashore and strode to the French camp. Before a startled Baudin and his shipmates, the intruding soldiers in red jackets ran the Union Jack upside down up a tree. They fired three volleys from their muskets. Their leader, Lt. Charles Robbins, led three cheers and claimed the whole island for England. Then they took down the flag and sailed off. Baudin described it as a "childish ceremony". A monument to it is at **Naracoopa.**

A passing ship's captain had named the place a year earlier, not after his King George III but his Governor King in Sydney. Dutchman Abel Tasman, incidentally, named Van Diemen's Land after *his* governor.

Perhaps 100 ships were wrecked on King Island's west coast in the 1800s and 1900s. The first permanent settlers arrived in 1855. The pretty but windy isle of 2,500 residents produces magnificent cheeses and beef and has an industry harvesting kelp for alginates. This is mostly exported to Scotland and used to make more than 1,000 products including ice cream, dyes, plastics and explosives.

King Island has full visitor facilities and historically fascinating features that can be explored in a few days. One is Australia's tallest lighthouse, at Cape Wickham. It was built in 1861 following the deaths of 400 people in the 1845 wreck of *Cataraqui*, still rated as Australia's worst shipwreck. See, too, the steel lighthouse at the island's 'capital' **Currie**. The former lighthouse keeper's house is the King Island Museum. The old scheelite mine at **Grassy** is also well worth inspecting.

***

RESUMING OUR TOUR, about 15 kms west of Wynyard on the Bass Highway through more farmland oozing with fertility, an attractive little resort with a beach-side restaurant is at **Boat Harbour**. Other such holiday spots on this tempting coast include **Sister Beach**.

Further west is the Sisters Hills, barely noticeable on today's highway. But before 1956 it was a horror stretch of gravel that tortuously snaked around the hills and took an hour to get through. The most notorious part of it, The Devil's Elbow, is still signposted.

At the top of the rise at **Rocky Cape** in fair weather what looks like a sodding great loaf of bread floating on the sea ahead at the end of a long peninsula is The Nut, the giant geological freak presiding over **Stanley**. When he sighted it from the sea, Matthew Flinders called it "a cliffy round hump resembling a Christmas cake".

A rewarding little diversion first, though, is to turn right at the service station at Rocky Cape and take a four-km trip on the fair gravel road to near the tip of this rugged three-peak wonder. The coastal views on either side are marvellous and you can stroll in a few minutes to what was a Aborigines' cave shelter.

Past the resort of **Crayfish Creek**, crushed iron ore is piped from a mine at Savage River, some 50 km south, for pelletising and loading on ships at the ugly looking mill and long jetty at **Port Latta**. Latta, by the way, is what the Aborigines called ore of iron, although they never learned how to make use of it.

The water of Black River, farther on, is stained darker than most Tasmanian streams by peat. Upstream was once the scene of an isolated timber-getters' settlement, infamous for its wild, boozy ways. Its 1854 Pig and Whistle Inn was legendary.

The notorious Pig and Whistle tavern in 1902 at the notorious, now vanished, timber-getting hamlet upstream at Black River. Drawn by W. D. Bowerman.

You are now entering the big municipality of Circular Head, the name Flinders and Bass gave The Nut. A junction on the Bass Highway turns left to the old farming village of **Forest**. Rather than continuing ahead to Smithton (which our Tour goes to later) turn right for the seven-km trip to astonishing **Stanley**.

An early sight as you drive in is the row of houses strung like a necklace, as if clinging to the base of the sheer monolith dominating this most picturesque of Tasmanian towns. Its salty, seafaring character is unique in the nation. Later, do take the steep path or the chairlift, like 35,000 others every year, for an awesome walk around its flattish, circular top that was a forest when white settlers disturbed members of the Peerapper tribe here in 1826. This was long before any other white settlement in the north-west and accessible only by sea.

Beach haulage. Bullocks lugging logs at high tide along Tatlow's Beach for milling in Stanley, late 1800s. The beach then was easier to travel on than the road into town. Colin Dennison Collection.

A mini valley on The Nut has a coppice. Peregrine falcons and hundreds of mutton birds nest by the north-western cliffs of the National Parks and Wildlife Reserve, which was free of gorse when it was farmed. The Nut is a volcanic plug spewed in a column of lava from the earth's magma 13 million years ago. It settled at ground level. The Nut's hard basalt did not wear away over the eons like the rest of the firmament.

Signposted to the left as you drive into town, the council's Circular Head Visitor Information Centre is at your service. Importantly for history buffs, visit the Discovery Museum at the top of the main street, Church Street, in the hall beside the 1887 St Paul's Anglican church, replacing an earlier stone structure.

Author Marguerite Eldridge has led a team of volunteers compiling and running the museum for 36 years. It is a captivating capsule recording the officially Historic Town's colourful events and characters over the years. It is opposite Providore 24, a unique supplier for we tourers.

Stanley is Michael Tatlow's childhood hometown and the seat of his ancestors. Apart from owning a farm on the Green Hills you passed as you drove in, Tatlows once operated at least two taverns, a blacksmithing shop and stables and ran a pioneering horse-drawn coach service to and from Burnie. They toughened their racing trotters by working them on the coaches, which ran along the 5-km shallow beach leading into town before there was a decent track.

Tatlows Beach is interwoven with Stanley's history. Many proud ships were swept ashore there in raging easterlies that sometimes buffet the town. In 1935, 280 pilot (!) whales were beached and died there, twitching noses for miles around.

Since its timber mill was moved to Smithton in recent years, dwindling the resident population to about 600, Stanley has depended mainly on tourism, wharf traffic, a busy little fishing fleet and farming. Visitors quadru-

Another whale on Tatlow's Beach. Mike Tatlow's late uncle, Jim Freeburgh, an old salt, inspecting it in the 1930s with his Whippet ute. Marguerite Eldridge collection.

The Old VDL Co. Wharf in 1858, the VDL store on the right, the former Bay View Hotel to its upper left and the Nut with some trees on top, remnants of a forest. Some logs are strewn on the rock face, destined for the mill. Photo courtesy Marguerite Eldridge, Stanley's Discovery Museum. Photo, Henry Frith.

*Tatlow's Royal Mail coach about to set out for Burnie c. 1908
from the Union (now Stanley) Hotel.*

ple the population in summer, filling scores of colonial-style cottage b. & bs, a big camping and cabin ground at Tatlows (the bottom) Beach, several motels and the solitary pub, the historic Stanley Hotel, formerly the Union (1849). Three former hotels survive: the 1842 Commercial Hotel, the 1842 Plough Inn and the 1849 Bay View Hotel. Fine restaurants include Stanley's on the Bay, once the Van Diemen's Land Company bond store built in 1835 supposedly from stone brought here as ships' ballast. The bluestone two-storey building across the street, now a b. & b., was the 1843 Van Diemen's Land Company's store, later a butter factory, fish processing factory and craft gallery.

A simple restored cottage in Alexander Terrace behind it was the childhood home of Tasmania's only Prime Minister of Australia, Joe Lyons. It is open for visitors. Stanley's oldest private house, built in 1840, is Touchwood in the main street up from the hotel. It is now a b. & b, craft gallery and café. A Seaquarium with live fish ranging from salmon and lobsters to sharks is at the main wharf, from where seal-watching cruises leave.

Stanley has the distinction of being founded on privately-owned land. It was the property of the once-mighty Van Diemen's Land Company, incorporated by Royal Charter.

The settlers were employees and soldiers plus convicts assigned to the company, owned by a clutch of London businessmen and politicians to enhance their fortunes. Their influence got the company, free, huge lots of land in the north-west that extended to behind Burnie, 80 kms from Stanley, in 1825.

And, yes, this first company town in Australia was named after a politician of influence, Lord Stanley, the British Empire's Secretary of State for the Colonies, the colonial governors' boss. He later became Britain's Prime Minister.

Toy town. Mixed businesses, restaurants and a fishing tackle shop, in cottages under the Nut.

Every visitor to Stanley should travel a few kms west of the town by Godfreys (the top) Beach to the Green Hills. The majestic panorama in different moods of the weather over the beach, the bay, the town and The Nut from the crest of the first hill past the beach rivals the scene at Cradle Mountain as the most photographed view in Tasmania.

Past the ancient-looking stone ruins of early military barracks at the next corner is wonderful Highfield, which attracts thousands of visitors a year. It was the headquarters of the VDL Company and the residence of its Chief Agent. The buildings date from 1829. The outbuildings include a stone chapel near the house for the boss and

The VDL Coy's Establishment at Circular Head in 1832. Highfield, the building on the right, is now a showpiece for visitors. The engraver in England, trying to impress VDL shareholders, fancifully shows The Nut as a loaf-like island. Engraved by J. Arrowsmith. From James Bischoff's sketch in A History of Van Diemen's Land.

Above, Highfield today on the Green Hills. Below, In its elegant prime in 1851, the residence of the VDL Company's Agent. It had a European-style garden manicured by convicts and where peacocks, emus and deer grazed. Engraved vignette from Tallis' Atlas.

his family. The Parks and Wildlife Service, assisted by local volunteers, is close to fully restoring the property, complete with original colonial furnishings.

As you leave the property, turn left for a scenic circuit. Overlooking West Beach and North Point, you can usually see Robbins Island and the peaks of Three Hummock Island. Apart from its islands, of course, North Point is Tasmania's closest location to mainland Australia. Its former telephone cable repeater station that received the first spoken messages across Bass Strait in 1935 is now a superior b. & b. Complete the circuit along Dovecote Lane, past a tower for another viewing of The Nut, and back on Stanley Road to the town.

Many tales say how The Nut got its name. Your authors, however, have colonial manuscripts of 1851 and 1854, calling it The Nut. We believe The Nut was coined by sailors who mixed with the Aborigines even before white settlement there by abbreviating natives' names for their rock. The names included Moonutreker (sometimes spelled Moonatreker) and Monuttek. But perhaps its shape inspired the name.

Near the Catholic Church in Marshall Street, and superb old Hanlon House b. & b. which we like, is perhaps Australia's most scenic burial ground! It is above Godfreys Beach where foam-capped waves usually tumble towards the dunes, beside the road to The Nut's gift shop and chairlift. The tombstones will tell you a lot about local history. The Tatlows, too!

SNAPSHOT 1923

Wild Wave and the groggy geese

A COLD EASTERLY, howling around The Nut, was driving waves with sickening thuds against the foundered barque *Wild Wave* on the morning of Monday, June 5, 1923.

The gale had driven the 237-ton sailing ship across Bass Strait from Cape Ottway, Victoria, as she was taking a cargo of barley and rum from Adelaide to Melbourne. The square rigger was washed, dragging her anchor, on to the town end of Tatlows Beach the night before.

Many of Stanley's residents had run to help. They waded out to the foundering craft and formed a human chain in the dark waves for hours to help ashore all the crew of 10 who had been swept overboard as the winter wind screamed around the ship's three creaking masts.

An anguished Captain Nicholson, other exhausted survivors and residents including children freed from school because of the disaster, were still at the beach watching the ship break up.

Stores, timber, rigging and broken barrels from the hold were littered everywhere. Gulls, blackbirds and sparrows were feasting on sodden barley mounded along the high-water line. The last of the old wooden barques built in Hobart was fated to be a total wreck, taking years for her skeleton to vanish in the sand.

The barque Wild Wave beached in June 1923, rum and barley mixing in her hold and destined to break up and be swallowed by the sand.

The quiet crowd on the beach was joined by a lady, Miss Amy, leading a gaggle of 11 pet geese and Godfrey the gander. The flock suddenly ran from their mistress, honking and flapping wings, scattering the other birds, as they attacked the barley.

The mature and single woman was quite a sight around town. Her black and white geese, led by Godfrey, strode in close company when she went shopping. Any dog foolish enough to come close was seen off, yelping from pain.

Miss Amy was thrilled about this free feasting for her flock. It was nearly an hour before she could herd the sated birds, wobbling with bloated bellies, several blocks to her home. Not that it prevented them from raiding more sodden barley from *Wild Wave* taken to the yard at the Union Hotel for the pub's fowls and ducks.

Soon after their arrival home, all the geese and the gander flopped to unconsciousness. A worried Miss Amy checked a few of them. Her pets, she decided grimly, were dead. That barley must have been poisoned.

But Miss Amy, it seems, was a thrifty one who knew how to turn adversity to profit. For there was always a ready market for goose feathers, for stuffing mattresses and pillows. And, of course, people would pay handsomely for a baked goose.

A neighbour heard her in the back yard weeping. He looked over the fence and saw Miss Amy tearfully plucking a goose. Several naked birds lay nearby.

The iron oven was warming, the dozen birds had been plucked clean, the feathers were packed in a sugar bag, when Godfrey the defeathered gander, the big master of the gaggle, stirred and squawked as if he had a sore head. Miss Amy's reaction is not known. We guess she was bewildered.

It turned out that Godfrey and co. had passed out, drunk. Near to dead drunk. Drunk from some 50 gallons of Adelaide rum that had burst from barrels in *Wild Wave's* hold and saturated the cargo of bagged barley before the bags had burst and the barley washed out to the beach. A ready boozy banquet, it was, for the local birds.

People reported that other feathered feasters had acted oddly, some dropping drunkenly from the sky.

Miss Amy spared her loyal pets from the oven. We can report with authority that she kept them in her home for days, sheltering from the winter chill, while she knitted, and knitted. She was seen around the streets of Stanley for weeks afterwards leading her flock as feathers grew. Godfrey the gander was in red. 11 geese were dressed in nifty woollen jackets of green, yellow, pink and blue.

NOTE: Your authors did not let some facts get in the way of this good story. For instance, Godfrey's birds might have got drunk on the barley at the pub.

Godfreys Beach and the township from the Green Hills, one of the most photographed scenes in Tasmania.

PART SIXTEEN 190 km
Smithton, Burnie, Penguin, Ulverstone, Devonport

Plus side-trips to Gunns Plains, Railton, Sheffield, Promised Land, Paradise & Nowhere Esle

A DRIVE of 12 kms on the Bass Highway from the Stanley turn-off past some flat bushland and rich mainly dairy farms takes you to busy **Smithton** on the Duck River.

It is the staging town for adventure trips to the island's most north-west point and the wild northern parts of Tasmania's west coast. Some of the west is in the largely protected Tarkine wilderness, claimed to be the nation's biggest temperate rainforest. Parts of its 447,000 hectares look as they probably did when Tasmania was part of Gondwana millions of years ago.

The pioneering Roaring Forties Wind Farm at Woolnorth, north-west of Smithton, generating power from the prevailing winds that sweep across the Great Southern Ocean from South America. A weather station here measures the purest air in the world. Photo courtesy Tall Timbers.

The beginnings of Marrawah, late 1800s. The main building here was a cheese factory. Colin Dennison Collection.

Forested Circular Head has a proud heritage of timber getting and milling. These chaps are taking a break in the early 1900s by their steam-powered log hauler. Colin Dennison Collection.

It is named after the Tarkiner band of Aborigines who, with other bands, lived in the far north-west for thousands of years. Rock carvings with designs strikingly like those in central Australia have been found west of Smithton at Mount Cameron West.

Smithton's rich history was fuelled by the timber industry and later farming. It is well illustrated at the Circular Head Heritage Centre on the corner of King and Nelson Streets. Swamplands south and west of Smithton still yield the best quality blackwood in the island. Areas cleared of them have become some of the nation's most productive dairy farms. Go up King Street, left along Tatlow Street and right into Smith Street to the Tier Hill lookout for marvellous views of the town, the estuary, farmland and forests.

The town's standout magnet for visitors amid gardens and its own little lakes with a thriving flock of ducks is the Tall Timbers accommodation and dining resort on Scotchtown Road. Tall Timbers is the take-off point for a host of helicopter and tough-terrain drive tours to some of the world's best wild frontiers.

Perhaps the district's most popular attraction is Forestry Tasmania's Tarkine Forest Adventures at Dismal Swamp, a magical place where you can walk or take a 110-metre slide from the visitors' centre into the world's only blackwood forest sinkhole. There are also night-time wildlife tours. Dismal Swamp was named by wet, cold and miserable pioneer explorers. It is about thirty minutes' drive from Smithton on the A2 Bass Highway, which continues to the coast at **Marrawah**.

This is a prosperous farming district with a beach that attracts surfers from around the world to ride on giant waves from the Great Southern Ocean. A further 15 km on is the coastal shack settlement of **Arthur River**, named after the infamous hanging Governor, of course. It is near the mouth of the river and by the Arthur-Pieman Conservation Area. Cruises upstream into the wilds leave from Arthur River. South of here is the Tarkine.

About 40 km west of Smithton is interestingly-named Cape Grim, the island's most north-westerly spot. Historic **Woolnorth** here (with visitor accommodation) is the only surviving VDL Co. land grant. It is now a 22,000-hectare dairy farm owned by New Zealand interests. Winds sweep in here to the Roaring Forties Wind Farm where giant rotors generate electricity. They harness the world's purest air, which has been monitored since 1976 by the Cape Grim Baseline Air Pollution Station. This lonely coastline can be awesome. Accounts of it vary, but it seems that VDL Co. shepherds in 1829 shot and tossed a few Aborigines off coastal cliffs here to their deaths in reprisal for the natives' driving of 100 prized sheep over a cliff at Cape Grim.

Exploring the ferny rain forest of the Tarkine, south of Marrawah. Courtesy, Tall Timbers.

On the way back east from Smithton towards Burnie, a rewarding quick side-trip to the right only a few kms from Smithton is to visit one-store **Irishtown**. The dairy farms here expanded from a little spread cut from the forest by Patrick O'Halloran and his wife Bridget in the 1850s. They trekked in from Stanley after serving their sentences as convicts. Patrick had been banished to the colony for 10 years for stealing two geese from an English land-grabber in Ireland. Freed convicts, incidentally, were not provided with tickets home. Half of Irishtown's few hundred residents today seem to be O'Hallorans, descendants of Patrick and Bridget's six sons and two daughters. They no doubt like the name of their haven, which some colonial clot or clown originally and officially endowed with the moniker Upper Duck Creek.

Back on the highway past Black River, you can find out how the pioneers cleared the forests at the Water Wheel Creek Timber Heritage Experience, in a splendid rainforest setting at **Mawbanna**.

Assuming you have visited Wynyard, a relaxing trip of 70 kms on the Bass Highway gets you to **Burnie** (pop. 20,000). The suburb of **Cooee** on the way to the city, at Cooee Creek, was reputedly named by VDL Company workers who heard this cry from Aborigines. The cry, lingering on the two last letters, was a native call of greeting and warning over long distances in several parts of Australia. It is also of course within cooee of Burnie.

The city is in sparkling transition from a grimy industrial centre in the second half of the 1900s to a sprightly commercial metropolis by the sea proud of its heritage and courting visitors. The Visitor Information Centre in Little Alexander Street attached to the exemplary Pioneer Village Museum is loaded with brochures about a host of attractions.

The Pioneer Village Museum is the north-west regional museum.

Spuds have long been the primary, primary product of the North West. This proud advertisement was in The Advocate *newspaper about 90 years ago.* Colin Dennison Collection.

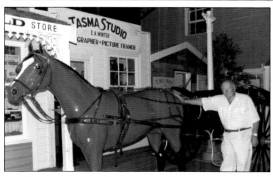

Co-author Peter Mercer at Burnie's Pioneer Village Museum, which he founded. The unique old Burnie street in the museum recreates everyday life in Burnie from 1890 to 1910.

Do explore its amazing collection. You are in for a treat. It recreates domestic and commercial life and times in the Burnie of 1890 to 1910, complete with recorded sounds of village activity. Here is a newspaper office, fully-equipped saddler's and blacksmith's shops, stores stocked with goods and fashions of the day, the Emu Bay Inn and even (a painful thought) a colonial dentist's surgery. This unique re-creation was the brainchild of its founder and inaugural director, co-author Peter Mercer.

Traditional and contemporary works are displayed just down the street at the Burnie Regional Art Gallery, under the city's Civic Centre. And explore the beach at Hilder Parade. We enjoy the fare there at Fish Frenzy. Other places to go include Creative Paper, where artisans sculpt amazingly lifelike people from paper and you can have a go yourself at paper-making. It is in Old Surrey

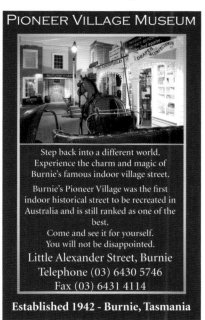

Road, on the way to the popular Lactos Cheese tasting centre. Burnie Park, which has a natural waterfall, has the city's oldest building, the little Burnie Inn (1847) saved from the wrecker's hammer in 1973.

The VDL Co. established the settlement, then called Emu Bay, because Tasmanian emus were seen there on grassy Blackman's Point in 1827. It was the sea outlet for the company's vast pastoral

The Burnie wharf and the bay in the moonlight, 1908. Hand-painted Valentine postcard, Colin Dennison Collection.

holdings to the south. Attention focussed on stocking Hellyer's "nobleman's domain" in the Surrey Hills. It was a disastrous act. Intense winter cold and nutrient-poor button grass caused the deaths of thousands of sheep and nearly bankrupted the company.

Emu Bay developed as a company town, like Stanley. Some 15 years after the VDL Company's arrival it was surveyed and renamed in 1842 after company director William Burnie. But it was still known as just The Bay until the early 1900s. Stifled by company restrictions, there were still only 200 residents 35 years on. Clearing the dense forests south of the town was slow but this was where the rich land lay.

Fortunes changed in the 1880s when Burnie became a deep-water port. It gained a rail connection to the mighty Mount Bischoff tin mine, to tap the great minerals mining bonanza on the West Coast. As mine production declined at Zeehan from about 1915, Burnie became increasingly reliant on farming and timber milling. Then, in 1938, because of its excellent port, Burnie took a leap into secondary industry. Associated Pulp and Paper Mills' new operation by the seashore ignited a doubling of the population from a pre-APPM 4,000 to some 20,000 by 1988 when Burnie became a city. But rank and polluting fumes from the mill sometimes embowered the town when Michael Tatlow was a cadet journalist at *The Advocate* in the late 1950s.

Burnie's deep-water port is operated by TasPorts and the mill by Australian Paper. The old and smelly pulp plant closed and paper production was scaled back late in the 1990s. Then came the transition, Burnie's third era; a wide-ranging clean-up, general city enhancement and the development of attractions for tourists it has today.

Remember that we are motoring, seeing the sights. So, after following the Bass Highway east from Burnie past Chasm Creek, over the pretty Blythe River at **Heybridge**, turn left at the traffic roundabout into Preservation Drive at **Howth** to go through wrongly and unfortunately named **Sulphur Creek**. This lovely route, following

The railway bridge over the Blythe River at Heybridge, east of Burnie, in the early 1900s. Except for the Bass Highway bridge, the scene has changed little.

the shore around Preservation Bay, is the former main coast road. It takes you to idyllic **Penguin**, of 3,000 fortunate residents. But it was *not* named, many tourism promoters will be alarmed to learn, because penguins lived here. Honest! This place, Penguin, was originally called Sulphur Creek because traces of sulphur were found in the creek there. The settlement of Penguin at that time was where Sulphur Creek is now. Because *that* is where colonies of fairy penguins nested and still do.

The Royal Mail people or a draftsman of the day were apparently guilty of a right mix up with the post-marks and effectively switched identities. Perhaps they were Sulphur Creek people who preferred home to be called Penguin and pinched the name.

Nonetheless, today's Penguin exploits its name big time. Models of penguins adorn main street litter bins, and pictures of penguins grace walls everywhere, it seems. The town's three-metre Big Penguin looks across the esplanade at the Visitor Information Centre. The ferro-cement statue was made in Railton and

The three-metre concrete penguin of Penguin, which it seems pinched its name from the first Penguin along the coast.

trucked here in 1975 to celebrate the town's centenary. As a teenage journalist in Burnie long before the coming of the Big Penguin, Michael Tatlow reported the alarming news that a bevy of life-sized concrete penguins that graced the esplanade had vanished overnight. Most locals were stunned. Some joked that the statues had swum away. Clueless police sleuthed busily. The little critters turned up a couple of weeks later 12 km along the coast, lazing on the beach at Ulverstone.

Timber splitters supplying gold-frenzied Victoria first settled and began clearing thick forest at what is now Penguin in the late 1850s. Their cargoes were taken by rowboats to small trading ships anchored offshore before a jetty was built at Penguin Creek. For decades only rough tracks connected the settlement with Burnie and Ulverstone.

The Silver Mines at Penguin, about 10 years after 'Philosopher' Smith found the valuable mineral near the coast in 1861. A steamer and sailing ship are in the background. Woodcut from the Illustrated Australian News *1870. From* Old Tasmanian Prints, *Clifford Craig.*

In 1861 James "Philosopher" Smith discovered silver-lead on the foreshore and iron inland. Ten years later, he found what was then the world's richest lode of tin at Waratah, visited on our Tour leaving Cradle Mountain. The first local farmer in 1861 was Edward Beecroft, who later built and skippered from Penguin a trading ketch named *Penguin*.

The town was proclaimed Penguin in 1875 and prospered as a rural and timber trading centre. But the coming of the railway in

1901 ended its days as a port. The Penguin History Group welcomes visitors at the restored old railway station.Proud residents there have enhanced the scenery with flowers and shrubbery on both sides of the old coast road as you leave east of the town by the shoreline. A little further on you come to a magnificent stretch of coastline. Around the point are the picturesque Three Sisters, small islands which are a rookeries for seagulls. On the right among old English trees is Lonah, a grand residence built in 1877 by retired British Indian Army officer, General Lodder.

A little further on is **Ulverstone** (pop. 10,000) on the Leven River. It was named after Ulverstone in England after being called Leven (1826), Badger Plains, Port Fenton and Cotton. Just as you have crossed the bridge, before you is a monument to Australians who fought for King and Country in the Boer War in Africa, 1899-1902.

Turn left at the bridge, then right into the first street on the right, Reiby Street, the town's main shopping strip. The big clock looking skew-wiff at the top of the street is a memorial to later wars. Its design was controversial amongst locals at the time. Turn right, almost full circle around the clock, to Risby Street, where the Central Coast Visitor Information Centre occupies the former railway station. Staff here can give directions to the big History Museum in Main Street.

The museum has an engrossing collection of Central Coast souvenirs of the past and heaps of old photographs and paintings. There are recreated old shops, a school class room, a post office, a printer, and premises of a saddler, wheelwright, chemist and a dentist. From here, take at least a look at Ulverstone's broad and long Buttons Beach. On the western end by the river is the Bicentennial Park Bird Sanctuary.

Much of this fertile area is well endowed today with farms growing vegetables and opium poppies and fattening animals. Yet, as we note at the beginning of our Tour at Devonport, pioneer explorers strangely considered it unfit for human habitation. Explorers venturing by land from the east quailed before the dense, towering forests on the way with no idea then of how to conquer them. Aborigines had been about, though, for millennia.

The settlement was known for years as The Leven after James Fenton settled by the neighbouring Forth estuary in 1840. Next came timber splitters who, like those in Penguin, shipped timber to Victoria. The district's inaccessibility by track delayed the opening of the first shop until 1854.

The settlement was grouped near the wharf until, like other places along this coast, the coming of the railway in 1890 injected immediate impetus. It moved the town's centre to Reibey Street. For 10 years Ulverstone prospered as the rail-head. But the extension to Burnie saw the demise of cargo movements from Ulverstone's port. Only fishing boats operate from there today.

SIDE TRIP

The Leven Valley and Gunns Plains caves

WE COMMEND to you a 25-minute drive south of Ulverstone on the B17 road through magical country near the Leven River through the farms of **Gawler** and **North Motton** (there is no plain Motton) and beside hop fields to the settlement of **Gunns Plains**.

A few kms farther south are the awesome Gunns Plains Caves, the major attraction in this centre of sink-holes and underground streams. You need to be reasonably fit, however, to negotiate the main guided tour's steps, ladder and low points in this enchanting world of limestone stalagmites and stalactites in lofty chambers. 54 caves and sinkholes have been found around here so far. Caves were opened to the public 100 years ago and now have brilliant LED lighting, claimed to be the world's best.

Gunns Plains has Wings Wildlife Park, a former dairy farm with a claimed 150 different species. But we have not counted them. A complex of other roads can lead you to the spectacular 400-metre-deep Leven Canyon at the river's headwaters.

***

REJOIN THE BASS HIGHWAY, which skirts south of Ulverstone. If you did not take the Gunns Plains trip, join the highway from Eastland Drive. Devonport is only 22 km distant.

This is a pretty stretch, passing by the popular holiday resort of **Turners Beach**, over the scenic Forth River to the village of **Leith**. The mostly farming centre upstream at **Forth** (settled in 1840) for many years was known as Hamilton-on-Forth to distinguish it from Hamilton-on-Clyde in the south.

The River Don Trading Company operated a colonial tramway between the mill and wharf at the mouth of the Don River (2 km north of the highway) and the great forests to the south. The tramway also carried limestone quarried at Eugenana in the 1860s for the making of mortar and steel. Some of the buildings at the once-thriving Don settlement still stand. The stream was probably named after the English brook of that name, not the illustrious river in Russia.

Devonport is explored in Part 1. If you began motoring at another location along the way, your Grand Tour of Tasmania is not complete until you return there. So continue from Part 1.

SIDE TRIP

Spreyton, Railton, Sheffield, Promised Land
With a dash of Paradise, Garden of Eden, Devils Gate and Nowhere Else

YOU WILL ENJOY some of the most marvellous mountain and farming scenery on the whole island on this half-day or so loop trip south of Devonport.

Turn right off the Bass Highway on to Stony Rise Road, the B19, and travel by **Quoiba**, virtually a Devonport suburb nowadays, and the once large apple-growing centre of **Spreyton**. Devonport Road

Hay bales in the lee of awesome Mt Roland, often capped by snow in winter, overlooking the rich farmlands near Sheffield, Promised Land, Paradise and Nowhere Else. Photo, Bruce Hutchison.

joins the route here. You are now on Mersey Main Road, heading for Latrobe, which is explored in Part 1. Turn right at Frogmore, west of the Mersey River, on to the B13 Railton Road. It borders the Mersey for a while on the 17 km trip to **Railton**. It is proudly touted as the Town of Topiary, a fun community of trimmers. More than 100 pieces of sculpted shrubbery are around the place to attract visitors like us. We saw a lot of hedge clippers in action during a stroll here cutting shrubs in the shapes of a Tasmanian tiger, a crocodile, kangaroos, Ned Kelly and a farmer with horse and plough.

Surveyor J.M. Dooley marked out the town in 1853. It grew slowly but the name indicates the momentous import of the day the railway came through the town in 1885. In 1914 Railton became the junction for the now closed Sheffield to Staverton branch line. The town took off in 1928 when today's Goliath Portland Cement Company took over from a small cement-making concern getting its lime from a nearby quarry. The grounds at the cement works, which has regular tours, show it is also a trimmer.

Sheffield, 12 km on along the B14 and past the Stoodley Forest Walk, answers Railton's topiary to entice tourists with extraordinary splashes of murals. The locals say the murals attract 120,000 people to town every year. The project is claimed to have also given Sheffield an appreciation of its heritage.

Just about every wall in the town, presided over by Mount Roland, sports a colourful mural. Most of them depict the district's history. School children have even painted mini-murals on council rubbish bins. The town hosts a Global Muralfest in March.

The municipality and other places around here are named after surveyor Nathaniel Kentish, who in 1842 was tasked with finding a route through dense forests from Deloraine directly to the island's north-west. But Sheffield was not surveyed nor settled until 1859. By 1862, 30 lots of land had been bought and the settlement had been named by a homesick pioneer. The first settler to build a house in the town reserve was James Powlett, from Sheffield, England. He established the Kentish Inn which became the Sheffield Inn and the settlement adopted the name.

Get directions at the well-equipped Visitor Information Centre, south off Main Street near the post office. Also visit the Kentish Heritage Museum, which shows off local artifacts and the history of hydro-electricity in the district, which has seven dams and seven power stations, built from 1963. The town also has a small tourist railway.

We urge you to be shown the way through the farming villages of **West Kentish** and **Roland** on the C140 to the world's most gigantic maze and the crazy model village of Lower Crackpot at mystically-named **Promised Land**. Brian Inder, the Laird of Lower Crackpot, turned his dairy farm into the maze, cockamamie model village, restaurant and lavender farm of 20,000 bushes over 20 years of creative work.

Promised Land happens to be a little west of **Paradise**, down by the road to **Nowhere Else** on the way to **Devils Gate**. And a place called **Garden of Eden** is hereabouts. To the near north

A couple of the characters we met at a main street café in Sheffield were local identity Ludo Mineur and his sociable companion, Pablo the alpaca.

of Sheffield is little **Nook**, perhaps named by a farmer who reckoned it was a good hidey-hole. Paradise was originally named Reuben Austin's Paradise after the settler who fell in love with this part of the world. Other religious pioneers around here, which some call The Bible Belt, named **Beulah** (the Bible's name for Palestine), **Promised Land** and **Garden of Eden**. We irreverently suppose a non-believer darkly gave the name Devils Gate to the site of Hydro Tasmania's big dam at a canyon on the northern end of Lake Barrington. The council regularly has to get replacements for the sign to **Nowhere Else**. A plaque explaining the name was also stolen. Now a link road, the track was a dead-end trail going to Charles Ivory's Nowhere Else farm from the 1920s.

Complete this loop side-trip by going back from Promised Land along the C140, turn left at **West Kentish** on the C143 past Nowhere Else and Devils Gate to the attractive farming centre of **Barrington**. Join the B14 here to motor back through Spreyton. Turn right to Quoiba beside the Mersey to Devonport to complete what we hope has been a colourful dip into this lovely island's past.

***

TO CELEBRATE our Tour, raise a glass to the tapestry of characters in this book.

To Martin Cash, the colony's Robin Hood; swashbuckling actor Errol Flynn of Hobart; Governor Lachlan Macquarie, whose name is so indelibly everywhere; Miss Amy, the goose lady of Stanley; Dame Nellie Melba, songbird at New Norfolk and Burnie who didn't make it to Zeehan; Captain James Kelly, exploring sailor who was jailed at George Town; Diego Bernacchi, the entrepreneur of Maria Island whose records of convicts were nicked by their descendants.

To Billy Hunt, the kangaroo convict of Eaglehawk Neck; the tragic child convict-cum-bushranger Tom Rares, to the Chinese miners and gamblers of the North East; to Dolly Dalrymple, the Aboriginal heroine of Latrobe; to John Bowen, the disregarded leader of the island's first white settlers … and to Launceston's writer and cleric John West, designer of the Australian flag who helped end convict transportation. Cheers!

*Cheers! Your authors, Mike, Peter and Charlie, toast the
tapestry of characters and amazing places on our Tour of
Old Tasmania. And cheers to you, our island's new explorers.
Photo, Tony Briscoe.*

THE EAST COASTER 1,385 km.

THE MAP OPPOSITE shows you in red the route of this tour of so
many brilliant parts of Tasmania, designed for a week or so of casual
motoring and sightseeing. You can hurry around the 11 parts in a
few days, however. The trips in blue are our suggested side tours if
you have a few extra days.

You will have relatively warm weather on the East Coast, thanks
to a nearby tropical ocean current. This Tour is a joy at any time of
the year compared with the risk of icy roads in the Central Highlands and on parts of the West Coaster and the Grand Tour in winter. The Tour can begin and end anywhere along the route but we
will assume a start and finish at Devonport.

The towns visited on the East Coaster are part of the Grand Tour
so you can find out about them and their past from the index.

PARTS ONE TO NINE. 1,170 km.

These sections are identical to the same numbered parts in the
Grand Tour

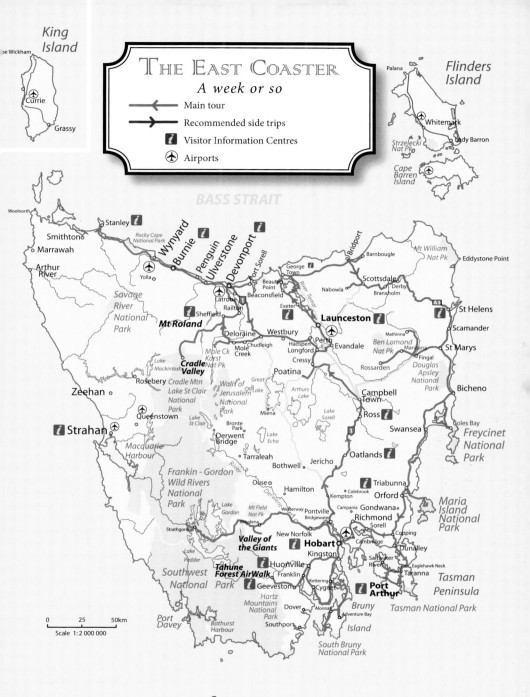

King Island

Flinders Island

THE EAST COASTER
A week or so

Main tour
Recommended side trips
Visitor Information Centres
Airports

BASS STRAIT

Woolnorth
Stanley
Smithton
Marrawah
Arthur River
Wynyard
Burnie
Penguin
Ulverstone
Devonport
Yolla
Port Sorell
Latrobe
Beauty Point
Beaconsfield
George Town
Bridport
Barnbougle
Scottsdale
Nabowla
Derby
Branxholm
Rocky Cape National Park
Sheffield
Railton
Exeter
Mt Roland
Deloraine
Westbury
Launceston
Perth
Evandale
Chudleigh
Hadspen
Longford
Cressy
Mathinna
Ben Lomond Nat Pk
Mangana
Fingal
Rossarden
Mt William Nat Pk
Eddystone Point
St Helens
Scamander
St Marys
Bicheno
Coles Bay
Freycinet National Park
Mole Ck Karst Nat Pk
Cradle Valley
Rosebery
Zeehan
Lake Mackintosh
Cradle Mtn Lake St Clair National Park
Walls of Jerusalem National Park
Poatina
Campbell Town
Ross
Swansea
Queenstown
Lake St Clair
Bronte Park
Derwent Bridge
Miena
Lake Echo
Arthurs Lake
Lake Sorell
Strahan
Macquarie Harbour
Tarraleah
Bothwell
Jericho
Oatlands
Franklin - Gordon Wild Rivers National Park
Lake Gordon
Ouse
Hamilton
Colebrook
Kempton
Triabunna
Orford
Gondwana
Maria Island National Park
Mt Field Nat Pk
Westerway
Pontville
Bridgewater
Campania
Richmond
Sorell
Strathgordon
Maydena
New Norfolk
Valley of the Giants
Hobart
Cambridge
Copping
Dunalley
Lake Pedder
Tahune Forest AirWalk
Huonville
Franklin
Kingston
Saltwater River
Taranna
Eaglehawk Neck
Tasman Peninsula
Southwest National Park
Geeveston
Kettering
Cygnet
Port Arthur
Tasman National Park
Port Davey
Hartz Mountains National Park
Dover
Alonnah
Bathurst Harbour
Southport
Bruny Island
Adventure Bay
South Bruny National Park

0   25   50km
Scale 1:2 000 000

© Walk Guides Australia

223

Devonport, Deloraine, Longford, Evandale, Launceston. 160 km.
Beaconsfield, Yorktown, George Town, Bridport. 220 km.
Scottsdale, Derby, Weldborough, St Helens. 165 km
St Marys, Fingal, Bicheno, Coles Bay. 85 km.
Swansea, Bridport, Orford. 120 km
Little Gondwana, Bream Creek, Eaglehawk Neck, Port Arthur. 90 km.
Nubeena, Premaydena, Sorell, Richmond, Hobart. 130 km.
Hobart to New Norfolk. 40 km
Pontville, Oatlands, Ross. 160 km

PART TEN. 75 km

Campbell Town, Cressy, Longford

This section follows the Grand Tour through Campbell Town but diverts to the *right* from the C522 onto the B51 road to old Cressy beside the South Esk River, then to Longford.

PART ELEVEN. 140 km.

Mole Creek, Sheffield, Railton, Devonport

As you have already visited the towns along the Bass Highway in Part 1, drive directly from Longford via Deloraine to Mole Creek. If you are short of time, continue on the highway to complete the East Coaster at Devonport.

However, to see awesome caves, alpine country and fascinating old towns, it is easy from Mole Creek to follow the road signs around magnificent Mt Roland to Paradise, then the mural town of Sheffield and the topiary town of Railton and join the Mersey Main Road west of Latrobe. Turn left to Spreyton, Quoiba and Devonport. This is also your chance to turn left near Sheffield to Cradle Mountain.

If you began the East Coaster at a location other than Devonport, continue from Part 1 until you return to your starting point.

THE WEST COASTER 1,795 km

THIS SUPERB TOUR, designed for an unhurried two or three weeks, takes you to every city. It goes through wondrously diverse territory that Tasmania has in such a compact way. Farming flatlands and lush rolling meadows, tropical rain forests, wave-battered and also demure coastlines, alpine lake country so often clothed in snow … you have it all. However, ice on roads at times in the Central Highlands makes parts of the West Coaster a bit risky in winter.

The Tour has 11 parts. You can begin and finish it anywhere along the route but we will assume a start and finish in Devonport. Nearly all the towns visited on the West Coaster are part of the Grand Tour so you can find out about them and their past from the index.

PART ONE. 160 km

Devonport, Latrobe, Deloraine,

Longford, Evandale, Launceston

See part 1 of the Grand Tour.

PART TWO. 175 km.

Launceston, Campbell Town, Ross, Oatlands, Richmond

This leg takes the historic Midland Highway south to colourful old towns such as Ross, mostly covered in the Grand Tour. See the index for information about the main towns.

Our West Coaster, however, travels south on the highway instead of the Grand Tour's north-bound journey in its parts 9 and 10. Do not miss the roadside silhouettes depicting historic events south from Tunbridge. Rather than continue on the Midland Highway to Hobart (which we visit later) and to see some fascinating old towns in the Coal Valley and also to minimise backtracking, turn left off the highway onto the sealed B31 Colebrook Road 11 kms south of Oatlands, near Jericho. This takes you on a downhill cruise of 45 kms to the famous Georgian village of **Richmond**.

18 kms along, the hamlet of **Colebrook** was called Jerusalem in colonial days. This is evidenced by Jerusalem Creek, just south. Colourful "gentleman" bushranger Martin Cash was once a prisoner at the Jerusalem Probation Station, the remains of which you can see today. Get directions from the History Room by the main street. Tempting side trips go to **Rhyndaston** and the lake behind Craigbourne Dam.

Continue from Colebrook through **Campania**, which has some interesting old stone buildings at its southern end, to Richmond.

PART THREE. 90 km.

Richmond, Sorell, Eaglehawk Neck, Port Arthur

All the towns on this leg are covered in the Grand Tour. Go eastwards from Richmond over the historic bridge to the sealed C351 Brinktop Road, then follow the signs through Sorell and Dunalley to Port Arthur.

PART FOUR. 115 km.

Port Arthur, Nubeena, Hobart

Follow the directions on part 7 of the Grand Tour to Sorell, then turn left at the traffic lights to cross over the causeway at Midway Point and past the airport to Hobart.

PART FIVE. 190 km

Hobart, Huon loop, New Norfolk

See the Grand Tour, part 8.

PART SIX. 335 km

New Norfolk, Lake Pedder, Hamilton, Tarraleah

Take the B62 Glenora Road from New Norfolk by the south-western bank of the Derwent River through hopfields at Bushy Park to Westerway. See the start of part 9 of the Grand Tour to be tempted

The wonderful and wild West

Chrystal, photographer Geoff. Love's water-loving hound, at Lake Rosebery, Tullah, near Mt. Murchison

Tasmania's highest waterfall, the Montezuma Falls, 10 km drive south of Rosebery near old Williamsford.

A stark sentinel of granite where the Tasman River flows to the Great Southern Ocean.

The historic Wee Georgie Wood train, now taking tourists from Tullah.

Winter always lays a white mantle over much of the West Coast.

**The photos on this page are from Tullah photographer Geoff Love's CD *Your Tasmanian West Coast Experience.*
geoffreylove969@msn.com**

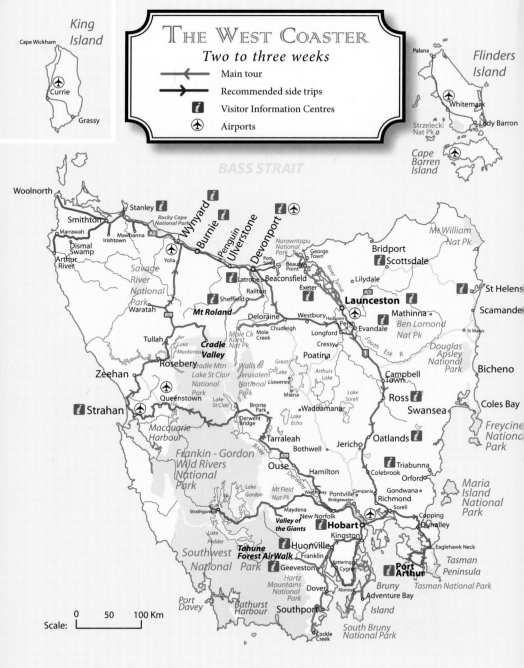

THE WEST COASTER

Two to three weeks

←——— Main tour

→——— Recommended side trips

i Visitor Information Centres

✈ Airports

BASS STRAIT

King Island

Cape Wickham

Currie

Grassy

Flinders Island

Palana

Whitemark

Lady Barron

Strzelecki Nat Pk

Cape Barren Island

Woolnorth

Smithton

Marrawah

Irishtown

Mawbanna

Dismal Swamp

Arthur River

Stanley

Rocky Cape National Park

Wynyard

Burnie

Penguin

Ulverstone

Devonport

Port Sorell

Beauty Point

George Town

Narawntapu National Park

Bridport

Scottsdale

Mt William Nat Pk

Yolla

Latrobe

Beaconsfield

Exeter

Lilydale

St Helens

Savage River National Park

Waratah

Sheffield

Railton

Mt Roland

Deloraine

Westbury

Hadspen

Perth

Launceston

Evandale

Mathinna

Ben Lomond Nat Pk

St Marys

Scamander

Tullah

Cradle Valley

Mole Ck Korst Nat Pk

Mole Creek

Chudleigh

Longford

Cressy

Poatina

Douglas Apsley National Park

Bicheno

Zeehan

Rosebery

Cradle Mtn Lake St Clair National Park

Walls of Jerusalem National Park

Liawenee

Miena

Great Lake

Arthurs Lake

Campbell Town

Ross

Coles Bay

Strahan

Queenstown

Lake St Clair

Bronte Park

Derwent Bridge

Lake Echo

Waddamana

Lake Sorell

Swansea

Freycinet National Park

Macquarie Harbour

Franklin - Gordon Wild Rivers National Park

Tarraleah

Bothwell

Jericho

Oatlands

Maria Island National Park

Ouse

Hamilton

Lake Gordon

Colebrook

Triabunna

Orford

Strathgordon

Mt Field Nat Pk

Wayatinah

Maydena

New Norfolk

Pontville

Bridgewater

Campania

Gondwana

Richmond

Sorell

Copping

Dunalley

Valley of the Giants

Hobart

Kingston

Eaglehawk Neck

Tahune Forest AirWalk

Huonville

Franklin

Kettering

Cygnet

Port Arthur

Tasman Peninsula

Southwest National Park

Geeveston

Hartz Mountains National Park

Dover

Alonnah

Adventure Bay

Bruny Island

Tasman National Park

Port Davey

Bathurst Harbour

Southport

South Bruny National Park

Cockle Creek

© Walk Guides Australia

228

on a magnificent 200 km return trip from here to the wondrous Valley of the Giants, the Mt Field National Park and a taste of the South West Wilderness at Lake Pedder.

Then return to Westerway, back on the B62 to Bushy Park and cross the Derwent to the A10 Lyell Highway near **Rosegarland**, where you turn left to see the old hamlet of **Gretna** on the way to historic Hamilton. You rejoin the Grand Tour's part 11 from here to Tarraleah.

PARTS SEVEN TO ELEVEN. 730 km

The rest of the West Coaster, its raw, alpine and picturesque highlights, is the same route as parts 12 to 16 of the Grand Tour. Enjoy!
Tarraleah, Bronte, Lake St. Clair. 80 km.
Lake St Clair, Queenstown, Strahan. 160 km.
Strahan, Zeehan, Cradle Mountain. 135 km
Cradle Mountain., Wynyard, Stanley. 165 km.
Stanley, Smithton, Burnie, Penguin,
Ulverstone, Devonport. 190 km.
If you began the West Coaster at a location other than Devonport, continue from Part 1 until you return to your starting point.

Snow-capped Mount Murchison from the lake at Tullah on the West Coast in winter. Photo Geoff Love.

You can find out about our other books and buy copies of them through our website.

Also available is Charles Wooley's rollicking recorded *A Walk in Old Hobart* for downloading to an MP3 player or computer. It's an absolute gem.

It's all waiting at

www.walkguidesaustralia.com

These dynamic new publications are taking the tourism scene by storm.

WALK GUIDES AUSTRALIA

Founded in Tasmania

Contact us as info@walkguidesaustralia.com

Index of towns on the Tour

Further Reading

Wooley, Charles & Tatlow, Michael. *A Walk in Old Hobart*. Hobart 2007.

Wooley, Charles & Tatlow, Michael. *A Walk in Old Launceston*. Launceston 2007.

Wooley, Charles & Tatlow, Michael. *A Walk in Old Sydney*. Sydney 2008.

Boyce, James. *Van Diemen's Land*. Melbourne 2008.

Tatlow, Michael. *Pike's Pyramid*. Hobart 2006.

Alexander, Alison. *The companion to Tasmanian History*. Hobart 2005.

Smith, Wayne. *Ripper Tassie Place Names* & *More Ripper Tassie Place Names* Launceston 2007, 2008.

Eldridge, Marguerite. *Historic Stanley* and *Stories of Stanley*. Stanley 1999 & 2007.

Hope, Anthony R. *A Quarry Speaks: A History of Hobart's Salamanca Quarry*. Hobart 2006.

Pringle-Jones, Jennifer & Joyce, Ray. *Tasmania's Heritage, an Enduring Legacy*. Hobart 2007.

Tasmap, *Tasmanian Towns Street Atlas*. Hobart 2005, 2006.

French, Greg. *Tasmanian Trout Water*. Hobart 2002.

Jenkinson, Mike. *Tasmania to the Letter*. Hobart 2006.

Your best general sources of information and free brochures and booklets about most parts of Tasmania are at visitor information centres in various parts of the State and shown on this book's maps.